Escaping the Shadows,
Seeking the Light

Escaping the Shadows, Seeking the Light

Christians in Recovery from Childhood Sexual Abuse

CONNIE BREWER

HarperSanFrancisco
A Division of HarperCollins*Publishers*

FIRST EDITION

Library of Congress Cataloging-in-Publication Data

Escaping the shadows, seeking the light: Christians in recovery from childhood sexual abuse / [edited by] Connie Brewer. — 1st ed.
　　　p.　cm.
　　Includes bibliographical references.
　　ISBN 0–06–061062–X (alk. paper)
　　　1. Adult child sexual abuse victims — Religious life — Case studies.
　　2. Adult child sexual abuse victims — Case studies.　I. Brewer, Connie.
BV4596.A25E72　　1990
248.8′6 — dc20　　　　　　　　　　　　　　　　　　　　90–55310
　　　　　　　　　　　　　　　　　　　　　　　　　　　　　　CIP

91　92　93　94　95　FAIR　10　9　8　7　6　5　4　3　2　1

This edition is printed on acid-free paper that meets the American National Standards Institute Z39.48 Standard.

To the most courageous people in the world —
our fellow travelers on this journey out of the darkness
and toward the Light of His Truth.

To those who are emerging as survivors,
and to those who did not.

Know that He catches each of your precious tears
in a bottle.

Contents

Acknowledgments

Special thanks to all who have supported this project in prayer. Although their stories are not told here, they helped make this book a reality. Thank you Arlene, Becky, Bonnie, Christie, Cindie, David, Diane, Ginny, Joyce, Nancy, Nick, Rori, Sandra, Sharon, Tim, Victoria, and Vivian. Without the help of Arlene Ussery, who helped two people with their chapters, and Diane Fillmore, who retyped many of the chapters, this book would not have been possible.

Thank you to Lonnie Hull, our editor at Harper, who understood and supported us. Thanks also to those people who allow God to use them in a special way in our lives — our therapists. A special thank you to Dan Haffey, who is accompanying me on my own painful journey.

My love and thanks go to my husband, Bill, for his emotional support and to our four sons, who wore wrinkled clothes, walked on sticky floors, and ate a variety of fast foods as the book grew.

Most of all, thank you Abba, Father, Daddy God for taking what the enemy meant for evil and using it for good. Thank you for redeeming our pain.

Introduction

"Murder of the soul" is how child sexual abuse is often described. You hold this book in your hands because you or someone you love may have been hurt in this way. In this book, twelve of us who were sexually abused as children share our stories and the hope we've found through Jesus Christ.

What becomes of adults who were emotionally and spiritually devastated in childhood? Those of us who move out of the darkness and travel the painful journey toward the light are called survivors. Those who remain in the dark remain victims.

Remaining in the dark might mean knowing that something happened and not being willing to walk the difficult path of recovery. Or remaining in the dark might mean refusing to explore memory blanks. Most of us forgot or repressed our abuse. A painful but necessary part of the healing journey is exploring these memory blanks: lost houses, rooms, or time periods. We encourage you to come with us on our journey toward the light.

Remembering our abuse, thawing our frozen feelings, and allowing ourselves to relive them is an excruciatingly painful process. But it is the only path to healing. We do not travel alone. Our Lord Jesus Christ is with us, and gives us companions for the journey. The writing of this book has been a part of our journey of healing.

We are in the process of becoming. We do not present ourselves to you as recovered; we write as people in the process. Our stories are from the hearts of wounded, healing people to the hearts of other wounded, healing people.

Twelve life stories are in this book. Some of us turned to "acting out": prostitution, homosexuality and sexual addictions. Others hid what was done to us behind a wall of achievement, perfectionism, workaholism, and excessive volunteerism in schools and churches.

We are people who once buried our painful secrets behind smiling faces, our wounds frozen with all the rest of our feelings. For some of us, survival meant living a lie, pretending that we grew up in a wonderful family and had a perfect childhood. Others remembered part of the abuse. But none of us remembered it all: our heavenly Father protected us by repressing the memories. We did not begin to remember until we were ready.

It is our prayer that by sharing ourselves and our hope in Jesus Christ, we can give you the comfort of knowing you are not alone. Though we may shake our fists angrily at God, screaming, "Where were you? Why didn't you stop it?" he promises to never leave us or forsake us.

The heart and soul of this book is the healing power of Jesus Christ. Just as he said to the dead child, "Arise, little girl," so also he says to the mortally wounded child within each of us, "Arise, little child, and walk." He is our hope and salvation.

How This Book Came to Be Written

Seven months into uncovering my memories, I attended a Christian Writers Conference. "Thank you, Lord," I prayed, "four whole days without dealing with memories."

But when I sat down to eat lunch, I turned to the woman sitting next to me and asked what kind of writing she was working on.

"Personal experience," she replied, her eyes holding a deep sadness.

Five minutes later we were sharing our stories of being sexually abused as children. This scene repeated itself at nearly every meal. Two of my contacts even introduced me to other survivors of abuse attending the conference.

I saved the phone numbers of the women I had met, but did nothing with them for five more months.

Then one day Victoria, a dear friend in a prayer and support group, said to me, "Connie, the Lord put it on my heart that you should do something about that book."

I also had a different book in mind at the time, so I asked, "Which book is that?"

"Oh, I don't know, just something about a book."

I struggled a bit. The other book would have been a lot more fun to write. But I did have all these phone numbers and a nagging feeling that this book needed writing.

An acquaintance in a writers' group called and asked why I hadn't been coming to the critique meetings. I told her I had been dealing with some personal issues. After much questioning, I reluctantly told her I had been sexually abused as a child. She told me it had also happened to her. That did it.

After pulling some ideas together, I called the people I'd met at the writers' conference, and we got together to pray about the possibility of doing a book. We continued to meet monthly to pray and to read what we'd written and get feedback. Now that the book is a reality, we are establishing a ministry to reach out to other hurting people with the hope we have found in the healing power of Jesus Christ.

Reading the personal experiences shared here may trigger memories. If so, you must seek help. Resources are given in a section at the back of the book.

If, while reading our stories, you experience any of the following symptoms, you need to seek professional help: nausea, difficulty breathing, a choking or gagging sensation, numbness, pain or other sensations in different parts of your body, crying for no apparent reason, shaking or shivering for no apparent reason, fear or rage for no apparent reason, brief pictures in your mind's eye, or nightmares that seem real. Professional help from someone knowledgeable about child sexual abuse is necessary to determine if these symptoms are an emerging memory.

If you ignore symptoms, or fail to seek professional help, you may instead have headaches or feel depressed. Do not isolate yourself! If it isn't possible for you to have a friend with you, use your telephone to tell someone what is happening to you. If you are not able to reach a friend, call Information and ask for a hotline.

If you are experiencing any of these symptoms, know that you are not alone. Even if you find it difficult or impossible to pray, Jesus is with you and will help you. Other people have been through what you are experiencing.

Our heavenly Father, unlike so many of our earthly fathers, loves you and will never leave you. He will bring people into your life to help you. They will not be able to stop the pain, but by listening to you and sharing your burdens, they will help you to reach a new and better place in your relationships with God, with yourself, and with others.

The journey out of the darkness toward the light is difficult. To paraphrase my friend Joyce, I only "write grown-up" like this on Mondays, Wednesdays, and Fridays. On Tuesdays and Thursdays you'll find me curled up in a fetal position, clutching my panda bear, screaming angrily at God, crying, and gasping, "I hate this shit." Having said that, I can say only one last thing: the joy found in recovery is worth the pain.

Note from the Author

Due to the fact that we live in a litigious society, my eleven other contributors have been advised not to use their full names. Lawsuits, no matter how ill-founded, can tie up authors and publishers for years, consuming vast amounts of time and money that might better be spent publishing helping books like this one.

We understand the necessity for this decision, but are saddened by it. We want to make it clear that we are not afraid of telling what happened to us. We are not ashamed or afraid of using our full names.

The responsibility for what happened to us is on the shoulders of our perpetrators. The shame lies with them, not us.

We will continue to speak out about what happened. No one else may know who they are, but they know who they are. We have told the secret we were not supposed to tell. Our last names may have been deleted due to circumstances beyond our control, but we have broken the silence. We have told. And we will continue to tell.

I

Surviving
the Darkness

Uncovering the Past

For Christ's sake, I delight in weaknesses...for when I am weak, then I am strong. (2 Corinthians 12:10)

I felt my jaw clench and my fingernails dig into my palms as I tried to stop the tears. Opening my eyes wide, I stopped the tears from trickling down my face. Success. I didn't cry. No one in church knew how much pain I was in.

My eyes darted quickly to either side; none of the other worshipers had noticed that I was dying inside. Good, I thought to myself; I don't want anybody to know. I don't want to look weak. And I don't want to make a fool of myself by getting up and leaving in the middle of the sermon.

Oh Lord, I prayed silently to myself, how can it be true? It's such a horrible memory. Why do you want me to know this? I don't want to know. *I* don't, but what do you want, Father?

When we arrived at church that morning, it was just an ordinary Sunday with the sun shining and the birds singing in the trees. As usual, my husband didn't come to church with us. But he and I and our four sons were going to a birthday celebration with relatives later that afternoon. I was more relaxed than usual because I was on a semester break from my job at the state university, where I'd been teaching writing for five years.

One of my sons was involved in the service that morning, so we arrived ten minutes early. I welcomed the opportunity for some silent prayer, something hard to come by in a noisy household. As I began, my heart was full of joy and praise for the Lord. But then, as often happens when I pray, my mind drifted. I thought back to something I had heard earlier in the week.

I had recently begun attending meetings of Adult Children of Alcoholics, a support group for those of us who grew up in alcoholic or dysfunctional homes. Following the same spiritual steps as Alcoholics Anonymous, we meet together to try to help one another and to learn to let God help us.

As I sat in church, waiting for the services to begin, I remembered the words of a woman who had spoken at the meeting.

"I was talking to my counselor the other day," she began.

Inwardly, I groaned. Oh no, another one of these really messed-up people who needs to be in counseling, I thought to myself. Thank goodness I wasn't affected that badly. Thank goodness I'm resilient, tough, strong.

The woman continued. "My counselor asked me about my childhood, and I told him I had had a perfectly happy childhood. So he asked me to tell him about it, and I realized — I didn't remember anything."

I remember laughing at what the woman said that night at the meeting. But I stopped short, as if a light bulb clicked on in my head. Thinking back to my own childhood, I realized the years between four and eleven were mostly a blank. I remembered teachers and the exteriors of houses we lived in, but little else.

Feeling remorseful at having drifted from prayer into daydreaming, I returned to my Lord. Father, is there anything you want me to remember about my childhood?

The services had begun by this time, but I was in another time and place. I was in the front yard of the house we lived in when I was a toddler. My Grandpa came driving up in his big black car with the running board on the side.

"Grandpa! Grandpa!" I called to him. I was always so happy when he came to see me. But this time was different. Instead of scooping me up into his big strong arms as he usually did, my Grandpa patted me on the head and passed by me to go into the house to see the new baby, my little brother.

In church, as I relived that memory, I felt the hurt and jealousy as if it had just happened. Lord, I prayed, how can this be true? I must have been only two and a half. Is it possible to remember that far back? Since then, I have learned that not only is it possible but everything that ever happens to us is recorded in our brain. I believe the Lord gave me this memory, which was easy to accept, because it was His way of helping me with the next memory He gave me — one that was extremely difficult to accept.

As the services continued, I stayed in private prayer and asked the Lord if He had any other memories for me. Letting Him guide me, I thought back to a time I was curious about. I knew that when I was three or four years old, we lived in motels for several weeks when my Dad had to do some work at the California state capitol in Sacramento. But when, as an older child, I had asked my mother about it, she had said there was no such time. So I had always told myself, If my mother says we didn't, I guess I don't remember it. But it was confusing to me, because I *did* remember it. So I asked the Lord about that memory and my confusion.

The memory the Lord brought to me was vivid. I was a little girl, sitting on soft green grass under a shady tree. My younger brother was asleep on a blanket next to my mother and me. The sun was warm where it shined down in little patches on the grass between the shady parts. The birds were singing on the branches above us. And the best part was the squirrels. We had a bag of peanuts, and when we gave one to a squirrel, he'd take it in his little paws, open it up carefully, and take out each peanut to eat it. They were so close we could see their furry little faces as they chewed. I felt happy and safe.

I thought we were in a park. But my mother pointed to a big, white domed building and said that was a very important building and my father had some work to do there. I know now it was the state capitol in Sacramento.

Then my mother talked about something I didn't like. She said "You forgot your toothbrush, so Uncle Malcolm [not his real name and not my real uncle] gave you one. He's a nice man."

He's *not* a nice man, *not* a nice man, I screamed inside. But I said nothing.

I wasn't in the park anymore. I was in church clenching my jaw to keep from screaming out, "He's *not* a nice man." I was digging my nails into my palms to keep myself from crying tears of rage. I didn't want to cry in church. I didn't want to appear weak.

"You're a *bad* man," I told him as I clung to the curved design on the screen door, watching and waiting for my mother to come back. "I'm going to tell your mommy [his wife] on you. And the police are going to get you."

He told me to come sit by him. I did what he said because I was a good girl who always did what grown-ups said. I sat down across from him, and he said, "I'm a good man. I'm a nice man. It was all your fault. You're the one. You teased me. Don't you remember you liked the part when I tickled you? You did a bad thing, but I won't tell on you. Because if I tell on you, the police will come and take you away from your mommy and daddy and put you in jail." When he had put his big man thing in my mouth, faster and faster, and I was choking and couldn't breathe and threw up, that was my fault too, he said. He was mad because I threw up on his legs.

So I returned to my post by the screen door and waited for my mommy. His mommy came first, and I knew he was going to get in trouble. But when I looked up at her and she could see I'd been crying, she looked through me as if I didn't exist. She went into the kitchen with the door swinging behind her. She called to him, and they had a yelling fight in the kitchen while I waited for my mommy to come get me. I traced the curved metal design on the screen door as I waited.

I don't remember her coming for me. But I remember the time under the tree when she said, "Uncle Malcolm is a nice man." My world turned upside down: because when my mother said those words and ignored the look that must have crossed my face, she confirmed what he had said. He was the nice one. And I did a bad thing, and I better not tell.

I didn't tell. I pretended it didn't happen. Deep down, I believed it was my fault. Even as an adult, when the memory of being orally raped first returned, I still believed that. After all, my mother had looked right at me and said he was a nice man.

Until that day in church when the Lord began to work on me, I never knew where my rage came from. I never knew why my uncontrollable anger kept interfering with my walk with the Lord. It was not until I began dealing with what had been done *to* me that I could begin dealing with the emotional, verbal, and physical abuse I had inflicted on my own children.

In my compulsive perfectionism, I would scream and yell at them to clean their rooms. Although I had promised myself I would *never* slap my children in the face as my mother had done to me, I found myself doing so, totally unable to stop myself.

But now that my repressed memories are emerging, I know the origins of my rage. And now that I have vented my rage in a therapeutic setting, I no longer have that bottled-up reservoir that would have been carried over to the next generation.

I've learned a lot about myself, my past, and the Lord's love for me since that Sunday two years ago. In learning to lean on the Lord, I'm healing. The Holy Spirit, who I consider to be my true counselor, is working through His people: my earthly counselor, the people I've met in support groups and my true friends. My best friend is my husband, who, since that day in church, has come to know the Lord. Because my relatives deny that anything bad ever happened to me, my friends in recovery have become my "family."

Soon after this incident of abuse emerged, other repressed traumas began surfacing. An ugly reality is replacing my pretend-perfect childhood: my alcoholic father and codependent, abusive mother failed to protect me from numerous perpetrators.

I still have many questions, ranging from those my parents cannot answer to the one question God answers with the Cross — God, why did you let it happen? Each day brings more painful memories of my lost childhood, but each day also brings growth, change, and a closer walk with the Lord.

Now I laugh at myself for the way I was before, looking down on people who were in counseling. In dealing with that childhood rape and other incidents I've remembered since then, I see that I'm not as resilient and tough as I thought.

The Lord is teaching me to be weak so He can be strong. He is shining His light into the dark shadows of my memory and, slowly, painfully, He is healing me.

ॐ

Abba, Father, Daddy God, I love you. I am scared when I see the evil things done to the little girl who is really me. I don't want it to be me, and I want the pictures and feelings to go away. I want to pretend my perfect childhood back again.

My denial is like a dragon only I can slay. My hand holds the sword that cuts through the lies and deception of the past, but you, Lord, hold my hand, and your word is my sword. Clothe me in your armor: truth as my belt, justice my breastplate, zeal my footgear, salvation my helmet, and faith my shield to extinguish the fiery darts of the father of lies.

Thank you Father, for sending your Son to us. Be close to me, Lord Jesus, as I slay the dragon who lies in the path of my closer walk with you. Amen.

My own story dealt primarily with uncovering the past, or peeling back the outer skin of the onion. I learned, and am continuing to learn, to be weak so my heavenly Father can be strong. Like the Apostle John, I want it to be no longer I who live, but rather Christ in me who lives. As God continues to reveal my past to me, I am learning over and over how powerless I am.

The concept of powerlessness, in my estimation, is the main link between Christianity and Twelve-Step programs. For readers who may not be familiar with them, there are numerous organizations, such as Alcoholics Anonymous, that are based on the Twelve Steps of recovery. In order to be accessible to all, they are not overtly Christian, but are rooted in scriptural principles.

There are Twelve-Step programs for people who need help with addictions such as cigarette smoking, eating between meals, or compulsive sexual behavior. "Sobriety" means the length of time one has been free of the unwanted behavior. As Paul tells us in Romans, "For what I want to do I do not do, but what I hate to do." (Romans 7:15) In Twelve-Step programs the key is to acknowledge our own powerlessness and to turn our will over to God.

Acknowledging powerlessness is also important in recovering from being hurt by others. Continuing to surrender to God not only my present and future but also my past is painful and difficult. When I cling to fragments of the past I always pretended to have, my imaginary perfect childhood, and refuse to let the light of His truth shine, I am in turmoil. As we say in Twelve-Step programs, if I turn it over to God but don't let go, I'll be upside down. I am still working on letting go.

The Lord is good. He gives us companions for the journey. One of my companions in recovery is Fred.

His chapter also deals with "letting go and letting God." He shares with us his double life: the nice, quiet churchgoing man who was also a sexual addict. Fred's life had grown out of control. Where did these compulsive feelings come from? Fred describes his recovery process as like "a detective uncovering clues." In this chapter you will meet Fred and see how he is learning that God can and is restoring him.

FRED

Uncovering
the Feelings

2

Surely you desire truth in the inner parts; you teach
me wisdom in the inmost place.   (Psalm 51:6)

Recovering the memories of my abuse has been a long
process, not unlike a detective uncovering clues to some long-
unsolved crime. At first, there were only one or two isolated
memories. By themselves, these clues held no meaning. It was
only as I gained more and more information that the pieces
began to fit together and retell the long-hidden story.

I was nine years old when I first began to hear voices in
my head. "You are worthless, you are bad," they taunted and
screamed incessantly in my mind. I lived with my parents,
sister, and two brothers in a nice three-bedroom house on a
quiet country road in the Northern California woods. To any
other nine-year-old boy it would have been paradise.

But I wanted to die. I lay down on the soft green grass of
our front lawn and stayed as still as I could. I closed my eyes
and let my breathing become very slow and shallow. If only I
could be still enough I could just fade away and never come
back. I could be free of my torment. I don't know how long I

lay there, but eventually I realized that I wasn't going to disappear, and I opened my eyes and slowly got up and walked away. I was going to have to live.

I could remember carrying that childhood memory for a long time but I didn't know what it meant. Why was I so unhappy? What could cause a little boy to act like that?

I work at a job that requires a lot of driving time, and I had recently discovered a Christian talk show on the radio. The host talked a lot about victims of childhood abuse. One day he conducted an interview with Jan Frank, who talked about her work with incest and sexual abuse victims. Strangely, I identified with many of the symptoms that she described. I too had few childhood memories, and had great difficulty forming and maintaining intimate relationships. Shame and low self-esteem dominated my life. I also learned that many victims don't even remember their abuse until they are well into their adult years. I wondered if this was true of me. This interview deeply troubled me. I filed the information in the "think about later" part of my mind and went on with my day.

Looking back on that time, I can see that God was orchestrating events in my life to lead me to recovery.

Some months later I began dating a woman that I had met at a church event. As our relationship developed I learned that she was a sexual abuse survivor and was working very hard on her recovery. As we got to know each other I felt an affinity with her and her journey toward healing. Somehow I could identify with her pain. At some deep level, I "understood."

Later that year came the tragic news that would be the turning point in my own recovery. I learned that my friend's daughter had been molested by her grandfather. I was shocked, horrified. Even more than that I was enraged! I kept saying over and over, "How could he do this to a sweet, innocent little girl?" I wanted to kill the perpetrator.

As I lay in my bed that night I began to sob uncontrollably. The girl's grandfather had taken something from her that could never be given back. He hadn't just violated her body, he had damaged her trust, her vitality, and her joy. He had plundered the very things that make life worth living. I was grief-stricken.

When I shared these feelings with my friend I was not prepared for her response. She looked me in the eye and said, "I know that you care for my daughter, but the way you are responding to this makes me suspect that you are angry at more than just her abuse. You are angry for you, too." She was right. Within a very short time I regained my first memory of being abused.

My first memories were just glimpses, momentary flash-backs. One day during this time, I was driving to an appointment when suddenly I was in another place and time. I felt little and terrified. I was waist high to a fat, naked man and his huge *thing* was right in my face. I was overcome with feelings of violation, powerlessness, and fear. The image went away, but the feelings lingered on.

As I continued to experience similar memories, I could soon place the house, the room, and my age at the time of my violation. I was beginning to remember. It was the same house and the same age at which I had lain on the lawn and wanted to die. Gradually I began to remember the man who had abused me. He was an older man who had purchased the house that we were living in.

He lived several hours away and wanted to retire in our area. He and his wife would come on weekends and work on the house. They converted a garage behind our house into an apartment for them to stay in when they came. It was in this little apartment that I was molested. He took me into the apartment and overpowered me. He would make me have oral sex with him. He would rub his penis on me and put it between my legs from the rear. One time he made another boy do this to me while he watched.

I still don't remember how he kept me from telling my parents. I recall that during that period my favorite kid goat was found hanging from a tree, strangled with his own rope. I suspect this might have been a threat. I'm sure that my parents' attitude about sex also prevented me from telling them. They taught me that sex was dirty and bad. If it was too bad to even talk about, it must be even worse to do it. I was sure that I was bad.

The images and feelings that were coming back to me were very disturbing and painful. I was having trouble sleeping and felt "out of it" at work and among my friends. At times my emotions would overwhelm me, and I would begin to weep while driving on the freeway. At other times I would be over-come with rage. I would feel violated if someone "took my space" in traffic or in a parking lot. I didn't like myself when I was like this. I didn't like being angry and rude.

I was also angry at God. I didn't feel that I could trust Him or depend on His love and care. I saw Him as an impersonal judge who was going to do His program with or without me. If I met His standards and did things His way, things were fine. If I didn't or couldn't, He would get along just fine without me. I felt very hurt and angry.

After a while I began to question my memories. I no longer lived in the town where the events had taken place, but some of my family still did. Over the Christmas holidays I went back. I wanted to visit my family, but I also wanted to revisit the scene of my molestation.

During my visit I drove out to the old house where I had lived as a boy. I slowly turned off the main highway onto the narrow country road. The redwood trees arched overhead, making a natural tunnel. Shafts of sunlight shone down, forming bright spots on the road ahead. I parked in a clearing and walked the last half-mile to the house. I felt more and more uneasy and afraid as I rounded the last bend in the road.

There it was. The house had changed in many ways, like the new redwood fence that had been added, but overall it was still the same as I remembered it—a long one-story ranch house with redwood siding and a large front yard, the yard where I had lain down to die. No one was home, so I entered the yard and walked back to the converted garage apartment. My feelings were extremely strong. I felt nine years old again. I was literally shaking, overwhelmed with terror.

When I returned, I shared my memories with my family. They didn't discount my story and tried to be supportive and comforting, but they couldn't confirm any of the details. All I had to trust in were my own foggy memories and emotions. But I didn't trust my own feelings; I wanted more. I wanted tangible proof.

My need for proof of my memories became a major concern. As I shared this with other survivors, they said I would remember when I was ready. But I didn't want to wait indefinitely. I began to consider hypnosis.

About the same time of my first memories, I had begun seeing a therapist. I discussed my desire for hypnosis with him. He didn't want to force the memories, but agreed to help me go deeply into my memories, taking me back to the room where I remembered being molested.

During the session my therapist led me into a deep state of relaxation and let me go back to the scene that I remembered. The room was there as I remembered it, but it was empty. There was no one in the room but me, and there were no feelings like the fear I had felt when I visited the house myself at Christmas. After the session I was confused and disappointed; maybe I was just making it all up after all. During the week that followed I arrived at a place of surrender about it all. I didn't need to know any more. I had tried as hard as I could to get proof, and I couldn't. I decided to work on what I did know and to trust that if I needed to know more at some future time I would.

Earlier that same year, before my first memory of my abuse, I had been brought to a crisis point in another area of my life. Later in my recovery God would show me how very much this broken area pointed back to my victimization.

Even though I had been a Christian since my early twenties, and I am now in my late thirties, my life had grown more and more out of control in the area of sex. Most people knew me as a nice, quiet, churchgoing man, but in my private world I was an addict. My "drug" was sex. I would use masturbation, pornography, phone sex, television, or whatever would visually feed my lust. Time and again I would try to stop this behavior and would even achieve some measure of control, but eventually I would slide back into the same patterns.

I was leading a double life. On the one hand, I sincerely was trying to live as a Christian, but on the other hand, I had a dark, hidden area that I couldn't ignore. The inner turmoil and pain were too much to bear, and finally it was enough to make me admit that I needed help. I went to my pastor and was brutally honest with him. With his help and support I made a call to a Christian therapist right there from his office.

During the early days in counseling I came across a book that would bring me new understanding: *Out of the Shadows*, by Patrick Carnes. In it I learned that there was a name for my struggle. I had a sexual addiction. I also learned that there were many others who had gone through what I was experiencing and had found recovery through specialized Twelve-Step groups.

I gained another very important insight through this book. From his research, Patrick Carnes believes that as many as 80 percent of the men with my level of addiction were sexually abused as children. This information added another major piece to my puzzle.

I continued with my counseling, and after getting to know me and my story my therapist confirmed that there was a very good chance that I had indeed been molested as a boy. As we worked with some issues from my family and childhood and I could begin to see some integrity and stability forming in my life, my sexual behavior diminished in intensity but still did not completely disappear. I was getting better but still had some major hurdles ahead of me.

It was at about this time that I decided to join a support group for male survivors of sexual abuse. I wasn't completely sure that I "qualified," but I figured I would give it a try. In my interview with the therapist who leads the group I was honest about my doubts and also about why I felt that I was a victim. To my amazement, he let me into the group. In the group I met men around my age who had all been abused. Some had been abused by their parents; some by teachers; some by brothers or sisters or other relatives. They weren't strange or odd; they were a lot like me.

In this group I found men who struggled with key issues of trust and self-esteem, and most, like me, struggled in some way with their sexuality. For the most part I identified with the men in the group and both received from and gave to the group process. From time to time I felt out of place and different, however—I was the only man there who could not remember the details of his abuse.

As God continued to lead me along the road of recovery, He began leading me to deal with my need to be honest with myself. I began to participate in a specialized Twelve-Step group for my compulsive thoughts and behaviors, where I learned to honestly admit that my life was out of control and that only God could restore me to sanity. As I struggled with this truth I eventually was more and more able to surrender myself to God. As more freedom and clarity came into my life I began to see that I had used sexual thoughts and obsessions to escape and to hide the memories of my abuse, to medicate my pain. I could now see that continued abstinence from my sexual addictions was the only door that would unlock my hidden memories.

I have heard emotional wholeness described as "knowing the truth about ourselves and knowing the truth about God." This has been the case in my life. By being totally honest with myself and God about the sin that was hiding my pain, I then could experience both God's removal of the sin and His support as I looked at the pain. For the first time, I experienced a sense of wholeness and integrity in my life. I was living one life, not two. I was facing life by God's daily power and not running away because of my weakness.

This renewed contact with God was needed because I was about to enter anew into the cycle of remembering and grieving over my abuse. Recently I attended my high school reunion in the town where I was violated. I wanted to talk to the family that had lived next door at that time, and during the reunion I found a woman from that family. I sensed God's timing in this encounter. The conversation was going well as we talked about old times and our childhood. I felt safe in asking her about the old man who had lived in the room behind our house. She became very still; her eyes widened; and she said, "I remember that man. He was strange and always after the little kids. In fact he even got my little sister alone in the playhouse and tried to kiss her." This was the same man that had molested me. I now knew without a doubt that my memories were true. I wasn't making it all up.

I am now in the process of living with my memories. Now that I know what happened to me and the reasons for the behavior that grew out of my abuse, I feel more alive than I ever have. My God and my loving friends are with me, and I no longer want to die.

Although my life is much better now than before, I am reminded that I am still in the healing process. It's not over. Something that happened recently at my support group for male survivors illustrates this.

Our usual format is to discuss current problems and successes and their relationship to past victimization. From time to time we leave that format and let a member recall and process a certain incident of abuse. I came to the meeting that night ready to recall and deal with a certain event in my life.

God had prepared the way. As we began our session, our group therapist, John, asked if anyone wanted to deal with a specific incident that night.

As I began to recall the time I was molested by that older man, I remembered the feelings of anger and betrayal I had toward an older boy who was also there. John asked if I wanted to speak to the boy. As I told him of my hurt and anger, I was aware that I was speaking in the language of a nine-year-old.

"I don't like you. I thought you were my friend. Why did you do it to me? I don't want to play with you anymore."

John asked me if I wanted to speak to the voices. Did I ever! I was now an adult and spoke in a firm and powerful voice. "I know who you are now. When I was little I didn't know who you were. You are evil and had an evil plan that worked against my life. You wanted to take a gentle and creative little boy and hurt him forever.

"My God is greater than you and greater than your plan. He found me and saved me out of your hands. I'm not afraid of you anymore because my Higher Power, Jesus, is in me and He is much greater than you. I hate you, and I expose you for what you are. In fact, my life's purpose is to expose you and your lies and bring others from the hurt that you did to me. In Jesus' name I expose you!"

As I was speaking I felt myself whole and strong in the power of Jesus Christ. I felt free and safe. The truth is out, and the enemy is conquered. Jesus already defeated him.

ð

Dear God, please be near to all those hurting men and women who don't yet remember the trauma of their early lives. Gently bring them to remembrance and healing in your time and in your caring way. I know that you are all-loving, and I know, Jesus, you feel our pain.

Be especially near to those who are trapped in the web of guilt and shame. Because of what they do they feel unlovable and even untouchable. They can imagine only that you hate them as they hate themselves. They are captives; they cannot set themselves free.

Jesus, you came to set all the oppressed captives free. I am one. I remember my prison. I remember the filth and stink. Yet you embraced me and carried me out. You washed me and helped me grow. By your love and power you did what I could not do. Through you I now live in freshness and life! Thank you, thank you, Jesus.

In his chapter, Fred used the word insanity *to describe the hidden and out-of-control addiction that grew out of his being abused.*

However, some addictions are so socially acceptable that they do not have to be hidden. Instead, they can be displayed to show the world how wonderful we are. These include workaholism, perfectionism, excessive volunteerism, achievement, and caretaking.

These were some of my favorite addictions, and those of our next contributor, Dan. His parents, like my own, believe that image is everything. His parents, like mine, have abandoned him and we are now a part of each other's recovery family.

The Lord tells us in Ezekiel, "I will tear down the wall you have covered with whitewash and will level it to the ground so that its foundations will be laid bare" (Ezekiel 13.14). Like many of our parents, Dan's had carefully built a whitewashed image that became more important than reality.

Dan shares how God is tearing down the whitewashed wall and replacing the lies with truth. Travel with us on the next part of the journey as Jesus, who is the light of the world, shines in the darkened places of Dan's past.

DAN

Uncovering
the Self:

The False Self

3

The light shines in the darkness, but the darkness has
not understood it. (John 1:5)

"God loves you and has a wonderful plan for your life. Let
me share what God can do for you. He will give you joy unspeakable, love undeserved, peace in tribulation, and a life
filled with happiness."

For a seven-year-old, my delivery was flawless. Sincerity
flowed from my very being. Could this be the day my two friends
would say yes to Jesus? I was overwhelmed with anticipation.

Yes, I did lead my two friends to the Lord. I had worked
diligently, day after day, striving to learn, and to learn to share,
the four spiritual laws, tools I would use for the rest of my life.
This memorable day in my childhood was the culmination of
that summer's outreach program.

This event would change my life forever. In the years
before, I had already learned to view myself as worthless,
strange, dirty, and alone. Something was wrong with me. It
seemed other kids would play with me only when my mother
bribed them with candy, cookies, or doughnuts. As far back as
I could remember I had been lonely and confused. I was not
really sure why I felt such pain.

But on that summer day, I set a pattern that would continue into my adulthood. This success gave me an identity that seemed to gloss over my dirty feelings about myself.

"My friends are saved!" I was so excited I stumbled over my words as I blurted out the news to my outreach study leader.

He was so proud of me that he picked me up and gave me the biggest hug I had ever received. Without putting me down he ran to his car, and in a moment I was on the way to a large Christian organization at which both my parents were top executives.

I do not think my feet ever touched the ground until he joyfully displayed me in the middle of the main office and announced, "Guess what little Danny did today?"

My parents, overwhelmed by his excitement, stopped working to listen. Within seconds, I was surrounded by every office worker in the place, hugging me, kissing me, and praising me for my accomplishment.

It's funny how kids learn things on their own. Prior to this time, I had never realized that in order to get love and approval from my parents, all I had to do was tell people about Jesus and bring them to the Lord.

After several days, the excitement diminished, and my normal loneliness and pain returned. Boy, was I proud of my parents! They loved the Lord so much that they stayed at the office seven days a week. I missed them, but I knew they had more important work to do.

After all, I did get to see them when our live-in nanny had time to take my sister and me to the office. My parents were important. Any kid would give anything to have a mom and dad like mine.

My dog, Winky, was my only companion—besides my feelings of loneliness, pain, and depression. I remember sitting on the porch holding Winky: at least he loved me!

How wonderful it was to see hundreds of people being saved because of my parents' ministry. My simple sacrifice of pain and loneliness was surely nothing when weighed against people being saved, praise God!

As time passed, I became the best Christian I knew how to be. The only shadow on my faith was the sexual desire I occasionally felt. I remember thinking it must be normal to have pictures of committing sexual acts with my mother swimming in my mind. Although I was sure such thoughts were normal, I knew that, as a Christian, I had to learn to control those disturbing desires. I had to put all filthiness out of my mind and never think such thoughts. Nevertheless, the recurring parade of sexual pictures never quit.

I was entering puberty at eight, which I also assumed was normal for my age. Now guilt too was becoming a constant companion. It visited me whenever I lay down on my bed. I was not really sure why I felt so dirty and guilty. I must not have read my Bible enough.

I excelled in both witnessing and Bible knowledge, the perfect son. At ten years old, I was known at our church as a spiritual leader. Even my peers looked to me for counsel. I hoped that the more I did for God, the more love and acceptance I would receive. If I just became a minister, then my parents would hold me and love me the way they had that one time when I was seven.

Between the ages of eight and sixteen, my mother tried to commit suicide seven times, but because I was the perfect son, I managed to keep her alive. I viewed her attempts as my father explained them — "just some kind of psychological flu that will end real soon — nothing to worry about." As caretaker, I wrestled razor blades and drugs away from her several times. I remember several other times rushing Mom to the hospital after she had successfully slit her wrists or overdosed on sleeping pills.

One particular time is set forever in my memory. This time Mom had overdosed and was passing out. My father put her in the car with me and my little sister and instructed me to keep slapping her to keep her awake.

We surely did not want anyone in our city to find out, so we drove out of town. As time passed, slapping failed to awaken her, so my father screamed, "Hit with your fist, harder! Come on now, harder!"

With my younger sister screaming, "Stop!" and Dad screaming, "Hit harder!" I trembled in panic as I hit my mother and watched the blood trickle down her face.

We ended up two cities away in a bad part of town. My sister and I stayed in the car when Dad carried Mom into the hospital. After several hours of waiting in the car, panic overwhelmed me. I feared my mother had died. I wrapped my little sister in the blanket, pushed her under the dashboard to hide her, and locked the car. I found a pay phone and desperately tried to call the only person whose phone number I knew, my uncle. Thinking Mom was dead, I needed someone to talk to. Just as I heard ringing on the other end of the line, I felt my body fly across the hallway and then my face slap against the wall.

Staggering to my feet, I faced my father. Writhing in anger, he screamed into my face, "Do you want someone to find out what happened? Don't you realize they will think bad of you? We will *all* look bad. How could you do that to us!"

He taught me well. After all, he was my father so he must be right. He told me again and again that Mom just had a case of the psychological flu and would be okay.

When I was nine, in between episodes of wrist slitting and drug overdosing, my mother would blank out and think I was her father. During these times, she would reenact past experiences using me as a substitute father. When Mom thought I was her father, she would do something to me I couldn't quite remember. But I did know she would beat me afterward.

She had told me how, when she was nineteen, her father had killed himself with a rifle to his mouth. She also told me he had sexually molested her. Years later, when the repressed trauma began surfacing, I realized that beginning at age three, she would lay me down on the bed and lick my genitals. She would then sob and cry, "Daddy, Daddy, why did you make me do it?" Then she would beat me.

At that time, however, I had blocked the memories of the molestations. I knew only that I had perfect parents. When I was ten, my father got a new job. Although he was no longer with the ministry, he was still very active in the church: deacon, Sunday school class president, board of finance.

I also had a lot of new responsibilities. We children were no longer cared for by the nanny the ministry had provided. My father honored me with the responsibility of keeping my mom from committing suicide. What a task that was! At age ten, I was so busy taking care of my mother I hardly had time to do the housework.

I loved Jesus, and as a Christian I put aside my own needs for the needs of my parents. I was afraid and confused. I really needed to talk to someone. My dad told me he would talk to me more when his work slowed down. He told me to wait patiently. I think he is slowing down now, twenty years later, because he is retiring. I have waited patiently, but I think it is too late now.

Without talking to my father I did learn, by example, one important lesson from him — that the most important thing is what other people think.

For example, I remember the time I tried to hang myself when I was twelve. I failed. The rope stretched, and my feet touched the ground. I felt dirty and guilty; that must be the reason I did it. But why did I feel so dirty and guilty? I remembered the importance of what other people think, so I did not embarrass or bother my parents by telling anybody what had happened.

Instead, I made up a story for my teachers about riding my bike and running into a clothesline. What a good laugh we had! No one noticed that the mark on my neck went all the way around under my hair. I would not want them to think bad of me.

As the years rolled by, I married and became a minister. What an opportunity to serve the Lord! In the depths of my heart, I believed that I finally would be special to both Jesus and my parents. Maybe I could feel secure and loved. Surely God would want to spend time with a minister, and what a minister I tried to be! Self-sacrifice became a way of life for me, constantly serving others. At times I even felt worth loving.

However, loneliness, guilt, and confusion still wrestled for control of my exhausted mind. Finally realizing that serving and slaving as a minister was unfulfilling and by no means profitable, I went into business working for my father.

For several years I managed many areas of my father's business. Each time I successfully completed an assigned business project, I would wait eagerly for my father's approval. Each time, to my bitter disappointment, I was met with, "Couldn't you have done better?" The carrot was dangled again and taken away.

I remember crying out to the Lord—Jesus, I am growing weary. Remember that first summer when I led my two friends to you? Was I telling them the truth? Where is my joy and peace? Tell me what is wrong with me; I can take it. I really can. Everyone sees me as the all-American Christian guy. If that is who I am, why do I feel unworthy, guilty, dirty, lonely, and hopeless? Who am I really?

Jesus, I prayed, I seem to be divided into two parts: the

confident Christian that people see and the desperate wreck that no one sees. I have done what my parents taught: kept up a good image and served others.

Jesus, I dream of you holding me every night; I feel your fingers stroke my forehead and feel your quiet, warm breath on my neck as I fall asleep in your arms. Send someone to hold me, Jesus, I am so scared. There are so many crazy sick thoughts of having sex with mom, and thoughts of killing my dad swimming in my head. I feel unworthy of your love. I am in so much pain that I do not think I can take another step. Help me, help me, help me, Lord Jesus, please help me.

I prayed a prayer just like this every day for three months until the answer came. It started with my three-year-old daughter being molested by our neighbor. I was so angry I wanted to kill the boy. Luckily, he was in jail, so I could not hurt him. After all, I said to myself, I know exactly how she feels.

"What am I saying?" I asked myself. How would I know how she felt? It must just be a father's empathy.

Over the next two months I was overwhelmed by other personal tragedies, including the loss of my job and the loss of a close friend. The perfect Christian guy began to fall apart.

The detective who handled the case with our daughter insisted we get counseling to help cope with the situation. That investigator will never know he saved my life.

While our daughter saw a child therapist, my wife and I would see Bruce, who later became my regular counselor. In our first meeting with Bruce I rambled nervously and expressed confusion in everything I said. I must have been easy to read, because Bruce called me three times at home to see if I needed to talk.

I assured him I was fine. After all, I was the perfect Christian, and I have perfect Christian parents. In retrospect, I realize that Bruce must have seen something in me that clued him in to my deeply suppressed emotions. My wife insisted that I see Bruce again. She became concerned when I stopped talking to friends and family.

She would find me hiding in the strangest places: under a table, in the bushes, in a closet. (These are the same places, I realized later, that I would hide after my mother sexually abused and then beat me.) When she found me, I would be spaced out, not really awake and not really asleep, just detached from reality.

Over the next two years Bruce helped me survive and deal with all my confusing thoughts. We never got to the root of the problem, but he kept me alive, and for that I am indebted to him.

During this emotionally difficult time when we were dealing with the aftermath of our daughter's molestation, I was sure my father would understand that I was not able to work six days a week, ten hours a day. What a shock it was to see the perfect Christian father being angry and vicious with me, his perfect Christian son.

I knew what he was supposed to say: "Take all the time you need to get well, Son."

But what he said was, "I need you to open another store next month." My father became progressively angrier as I became increasingly unable to perform to his expectations.

Barely able to function either at work or at home, I stumbled on, doing what I could do. My father viewed my lack of performance as a direct assault on him and his well-being. He would call me at my office at the beginning of every day and scream at me to stop fighting him. But I was helping all I could.

Then one day he shifted gears and started a new assault on me. He would still call me every day, but now I became a demon, devil, vicious monster, mother hater, and no son of his. I had no strength and was doing all I could, but he continued to attack me.

Where did the perfect Christian father go? I began questioning whether he had ever been there. Our image as perfect Christians was still intact. Were we presenting a Trojan horse, with our true selves locked inside? Could it be that we were not the people our image expressed?

My father was two-faced. He appeared to be the perfect Christian, attending church on Sunday, serving on the board of finance, organizing church social events, and substitute teaching on Wednesday-night Bible study. My father never used bad language and several times he even led the choir. But the rest of the time he was a different man. Not until later would I discover the extent of his abuse, which I had blocked out.

All my life I had been able to get love and affection by earning it; now I was emotionally crippled and unable to perform. It was at about this time that I remembered a truth out of my past: "God loves you and has a wonderful plan for your life. Let me share what God will do for you. He will give you joy unspeakable, love undeserved, peace in tribulation, and a life filled with happiness."

I was loved by God without my efforts; could this be true? As I looked at my own children and examined my feelings about them, I realized that I loved them because they were mine and not for what they did for me.

This truth opened my mind to other memories and understandings, most of which are very painful. I began questioning the form of Christianity my parents lived, the form that image holds more importance than who you are inside. As I accepted that Jesus loves me for just being me, I freed my mind to recall my lost memories. In the beginning they came in the form of disturbing dreams. Later they came as flashbacks in my conscious mind.

My childhood fantasies about my parents were lost forever with the realization that I had been abused and sexually molested by both my parents. It was not only my mother; my father was involved also. He forced me to have sex with his business partners.

I wanted to believe the false image my family presented rater than accept the horrible truth about my parents and my childhood. They put on a facade of godliness, but they were covering up the evil in their hearts.

As Jesus began to teach me, I understood that what my heart was inside was more important than my image! My parents were hiding behind their image and not facing the truth. Their real selves were hidden, and I became their victim.

The confident Christian I looked like was my false self. My real self, or what was left of me, was a wounded child torn with painful memories.

I was like the foolish man in the story Jesus told who built his house upon sand. After the floods of truth and reality had torn down my house built on the sand of image and the false self, Jesus mercifully began rebuilding my life on Him and His love for me. He is my foundation. Jesus loves me and has always loved me without me being anything else but my real self.

Working through the memories and the process of forgiveness is excruciatingly painful, but today Jesus is my foundation, and in His love for me do I trust.

❧

Father, I am not sure I want to face all the haunting memories which are surfacing every day now. I tremble at the ugly reality of sin in which my parents and others involved me. Sometimes I feel dirty and rejected. I do not know what it means to have a good father, so show me what a real father is like. Sometimes I am scared to talk to you and I am afraid of your wrath. Help me to know I am your child, your innocent child. Help me to feel loved and accepted by you. Help me know you love me no matter what has happened. Help me Jesus.

II

Struggling out of the Darkness

In each of the previous chapters, Dan's, Fred's, and my own, there has been an emphasis on uncovering the past. All of us had "forgotten" large chunks of our childhood. The psychological term for this is repression.

In my opinion, repression is a gift from God. A child who is being abused and/or abandoned by caretakers has nowhere to run. In repression, the mind protects the child by "forgetting" what happened.

In child sexual abuse, an innocent and vulnerable child is physically and emotionally invaded. Overtly or covertly, the child is told he or she is responsible. Because the child is unable to cope with devastating feelings and has nowhere to turn, no one to tell, the incidents are lost to the conscious memory.

But the feelings remain and come out in other ways. In the previous chapters, we've seen my uncontrollable anger, Fred's feelings of worthlessness and Dan's need to be "perfect."

In Toni's and the two following chapters, we'll take a closer look at the process of unearthing repressed trauma, discovering the "forgotten" past.

When Toni and I were in a group for adult children of alcoholics, we thought we recognized each other. We soon realized that several years earlier she had taught two of my sons.

We had a special bond, which grew even stronger as my return-ing incest memories triggered hers.

Because she is an artist, Toni's journey of discovery often takes the shape of sketches or paintings, sometimes on paper and sometimes in her mind.

T O N I

Discovering
the Past

4

He reveals deep and hidden things; he knows what
lies in darkness, and light dwells with him.
(Daniel 2:22)

"The trees! The trees are gone!" I cried in disbelief. I
pointed toward the back of a huge property that held six small,
neat houses. "Do you see back there where those apartments
are?" I asked a friend who was with me. "When I was little, the
most beautiful stand of pine trees was there. We even had a
playhouse. I can't believe the playhouse and the trees are all
gone!"

I felt an inexplicable sadness sweep over me. I had no idea
how important this visit to my childhood house would become. For in less than three weeks, the memories would begin
to unwind. I have not returned to see the house again, nor have
I ever told my friend what I have since discovered.

I had begun seeing a counselor recently because of several women I knew, including Connie, who were in therapy
and beginning to recover incest memories that they had
repressed all their lives. This triggered some very uncomfortable feelings in me.

"I'm ready to know. I have to know," I told my counselor in our first session. "I have this feeling about my childhood, and it isn't good."

I told her that two years earlier, someone very close to me had been violently attacked, raped, and her life threatened. Initially, I felt overwhelming pain for her, but strangely, I cried little. All my emotions shut down. I have not yet been able to truly grieve, though a part of me feels anguish for her still.

I had an awful feeling there was something I didn't remember about my childhood, even though I remember a lot. As I told my counselor, "Something I don't remember is keeping me from feeling the grief I need to feel for her — something that is keeping me from feeling a lot of things."

I could see myself at age two or three, dragging my two rag dolls around by the hair. I saw myself punching their stomachs so they would hurt the way my own stomach hurt on so many mornings. Why had my stomach hurt so?

"Constipation," Mommy always told me then. She subjected me to unbearably painful enemas. I felt violated, and I both hated and feared her when she inflicted them on me. I learned not to tell her when my stomach hurt. I just quietly lay down on the floor, and after a while the pain would go away.

The first memory I recovered was about the playhouse on the property with the trees, when I was about three years old.

The playhouse had just been built. It really belonged to my friend Carole, but it was going to be for all of us children to play in — all of us who lived in the six houses on the large property.

I saw myself one early afternoon just looking at the playhouse. I knew I was not supposed to be out of our own yard and down there by the trees alone, but I was there anyway.

Suddenly, from somewhere behind me came a stranger. I had never seen him before. He was very friendly, but I felt guarded at first. He seemed to move so quickly. He began to describe all the furniture that was being made for our playhouse, and he told me exactly where all of it would be placed inside. I remember that I didn't like it that he knew more about our playhouse than I did.

A few days later, Carole and I went to see the playhouse together. She'd said the furniture was there. We went inside to see it, and it was all just as the stranger had said it would be. I felt apprehensive for some reason, and oddly detached.

This is Carole's playhouse, I remember thinking. It's not really mine anyway. I did not feel safe being there, though I had always loved being down by the trees before.

On the way home from my therapist's office I wondered what could have happened. I don't remember. I don't remember. I felt so alone. A sweet-sad song was playing on the car radio, touching the pain deep inside. For the first time in my life I cried for the little child who had been me.

Knowing that at some time we would be doing art therapy, I began "thinking" a painting. Over a period of several days, it slowly took shape in my mind. I remember thinking, How can I even begin to paint something I can't remember? I imagined myself choosing a large sheet of paper, an inch-and-a-half-wide flat brush and green paint, middle to dark shades, also brown and black. I don't know why I chose green. I hate it. I have hated green for as long as I can remember.

In my mind, I began to paint. Curiously, I did not paint the playhouse at all. I painted wide, bold strokes radiating outward from a center — like a flower, like many flowers. That's strange, I thought, flowers aren't green. The upper three-quarters of the paper was mostly covered. Darker shades were in circles. An even darker streak extended out from the center — brownish almost, but it seemed to trail off and have no end. I couldn't tell where it went. I saw this mind-painting for several days, and although I couldn't make any sense of it, I knew it must be important.

A few days later, my mind-painting had changed. Instead of tempera, it was in watercolor on wet paper, and blurry. With a terrible sense of foreboding, I remembered. It is blurry because a three-year-old's tears blurred the dark trees above her as she lay helpless and victimized on the ground. Having pinned her down, the stranger had begun to molest her.

The trunks of the trees seem to have no end, for from her position she cannot see where they go into the ground. I know she went numb then. I think part of me died there. It is best that the trees are gone now, for they were witness to a treacherous thing.

I looked at this painting in absolute amazement, as though I had really painted it. It had unlocked darkness as though it were real. It changed again, and I saw a patch of blue. There *had* been sky; I just hadn't seen it.

"Heaven," my counselor told me later. "The Lord was there, grieving for you. He will redeem it for you one day."

The stranger had used his free agency, and he had taken mine. And yet, I feel my life has been guided by the Lord, moving toward recovery. I know now that He loved me then, even though He allowed terrible things to happen to me.

Then I became aware of something that had been there all along — or something that *wasn't* there: much of the lower left quadrant of the painting was missing. It was beige, and blurred so I could not see.

When praying for things to be revealed, I discovered, we can't always choose our time.

I was sitting quietly in church when I suddenly saw with clarity the blurred beige part of my painting. I recoiled in horror. I saw his stomach first, then his penis. I was being sodomized. For a long terrible moment I relived the violent thing that had been done to me under the trees. I wanted to cry out, but could not. So, as I had done long ago, I screamed inwardly.

My "painting" was finished at last.

But soon I began to remember other incidents. There was a foster parent the year I was six. I only remembered sounds at first: the doorknob turning in the night, and his breathing. I remembered the fear, and going numb.

The other foster parent, his wife, beat us almost nightly with a long, flexible dowel rod. Both of them were emotionally abusive as well. My mother left us in their questionable care for an entire year because she worked weeknights. But many weekends she did not come to see us. Finally, after my little brother was beaten so hard with a razor strap that I feared for his life, I told my mother about the beatings and she brought us back to live with her. I had already blocked out the molestations, but I do remember that it was during this year that my mother became an alcoholic.

When I was nine or ten, my mother was dating a man who had a violent temper when he drank. His anger terrified me. Once he and my mother took me and my little brother to a drunken party.

A lot of noisy people, including my mother, were jammed into the kitchen and livingroom of someone's tiny apartment. My brother and I had been taken into a bedroom and told to stay there. I was gang-raped by him and two other men. My little brother was forced to witness it. I felt destroyed. My mother did not know what they had done to me until it was too late. Then she went into denial. I blocked that memory also.

Far more heartbreaking than all of these memories was the realization that my grandfather, whom I had loved and I had always believed loved me, had betrayed me too. I have seen that hideous shade of pale green in my mind, and I know

now why I hate it. It was the color of his room. And I had been trapped in that room with him. Body memories returned. I know now why I cannot bear to have anyone's fingers touch my back: I had been held down that way. And anything brushing against my ankles puts me in unbearable anguish, because I had been gripped and dragged by them.

I have found photographs he took of me soon after he had begun molesting me, from infancy through age eight. At last I understand the look in my eyes; it is not shyness. It is pain going to numbness. It is fear, hopelessness, and betrayal.

I know now why I felt nothing when he died. Gramp had died after an especially long illness, when I was nine. Something inside me ceased to live. For all these years I had mistakenly believed that it was I who had killed him. I had borne a guilt that was never mine to bear.

Whether I am still at the beginning of my journey toward healing, or nearing the end, I cannot yet tell. Each time I recover a memory, I feel stronger and freer of the shadows that have bound me. The timetable is different for each of us: for coming out of denial, recovering the memories, accepting the past, and letting it go. Each one of us is unique in the eyes of God.

God gave me emotional protection long ago when I needed it, which let me detach and go outside myself during the nightmares of abuse. He gave me complete forgetting until I had found Him, learned to trust Him, and knew of His love for me. Then, using the courage of others like myself who were also beginning to remember, and through a few close friends whose love means everything to me, He began slowly, gently, and lovingly to help me unveil my past.

"Why do you do this? Why are you willing to dig up the past like this?" I was asked once.

"Unless the ground is plowed," I replied, "nothing will ever grow. I do it because I must do it to be freed of the darkness and the nightmares. I do it because someday I want to be able to reach out to another — to take her by the hand and give her the courage to begin to heal her own inner torment. It is why the Savior placed us here, to use our own trials to help others. And I want with all my heart to do that."

Recovered? No. I am only in the process of recovery. I have not yet been able to feel my anger. I flee from it. And I have never really cried. I have an unreasonable fear within me that once I begin to cry, I may never be able to stop. Until I travel through all of these challenges, I cannot reach the point of forgiveness. And it is forgiveness that will truly free me.

The Lord has given me memory as soon as I have been able to bear it. He has guided me through a wise and sensitive counselor. Through journal writing I can validate what really happened to little Toni and come out of denial. I have learned righthand-lefthand dialogue writing with my inner child, lost until now. And I have learned to render lefthanded paintings and drawings (real ones this time!) that reach into the right brain and draw out the truth, uncensored. From time to time, I have been given significant dreams.

I have learned through others who have given me the courage to begin this discovery. Most of all I am being guided by prayer and by the Scriptures, and through the knowledge that the Lord is with me every step of this journey out of darkness and into the sunlight.

&

O Eternal Father in Heaven,
Hear this, the prayer of my heart:

Gratitude fills me to know Thou art ever by my side, that Thou hast never given me more than I can bear in recovering the memories. Soon the forgetting need be no more, for Thou hast strengthened me — freeing me from pain that has held me prisoner all my days.

My prayer reaches out past the desires of my own heart, Father, but includes them too. I plead with Thee to help those of us who have courageously told our stories to now touch the lives of others through our words, that they may come unto Thee and begin their own healing. Let us listen always to Thy voice on our behalf, and learn to trust and follow Thee where Thou wouldst have us go. Help us to become whole — to release our pain to spring, where dwells the promise of a radiant sun.

These things I pray, Father, in the name of Thy beloved Son, Jesus Christ. Amen.

No book on child sexual abuse would be complete without mention of the fact that many people abused as children grow up and move away only to find themselves in other abusive relationships. This was Sara's experience.

After being trained as a child to submit to abusive behavior, she repeated that pattern in her first marriage. Like many victims, she thought she deserved nothing better.

In this part of our journey, we go with Sara as she leaves the victim role behind and allows God to transform her into a survivor. Though I haven't gotten to know her well, Sara is a prayer warrior and a sister in the Lord.

SARA

Discovering
the Feelings

5

You will know the truth, and the truth will set you free.   (John 8:32)

I rose from where I knelt and threw myself across the bed. My body throbbed with shame over my jealousy and anger. How could I be so unchristian? No matter how hard I tried, I could never be good enough.

I could still hear my husband's voice ridiculing me, laughing over the telephone to his girlfriend. The room had started to close in on me. I wanted to get away, away from his taunting. But where? In the closet. I'd hide in the closet. In the silence, crouched down among the clothes and shoes, I prayed that I would die. But nothing happened. So I thought of ways I could kill myself and solve everyone's problem with me. Memories of my past tumbled through my mind, validating my feelings that I was not worthy of life.

But where did these feelings come from? Although I would discover later that they had originated in forgotten incidents that had happened to me when I was very small, at this time it seemed that the problem had always been in me. I just wasn't good enough.

Good had been carefully defined for me by my father. It meant never causing anyone any trouble, such as asking them to help me when they already had problems enough of their own, or telling them of my own fears or expressing any discontent with my life. Such negative feelings were *bad*. I must be good like God — loving and forgiving others unconditionally, never angry or selfish, or I'd be bad like satan.

And I couldn't let down my respectable Christian family. We never acknowledged having any problems, at home or elsewhere. If we forgot, our angry outbursts or contradictory opinions were immediately stifled by my father's self-righteous silence. I never remember him letting his emotions get the best of him — except once, when in a rage he beat me. Shocked, I looked up into his face and saw a confused, hurting child. Shame overwhelmed me. I deserved what I'd gotten, but he didn't deserve the pain I had caused him. I determined I'd never hurt him again.

But my father wasn't the only one who needed me to take care of him. I saw clearly my mother's suicidal tendencies, my sister's depression, and my brother's desperate search for self through drugs. I knew I must forget my own needs, my nightmares of suffocating and of objects swelling in my mouth. I focused on taking care of my family.

When I was eight, my twelve-year-old brother began touching me sexually. My shock was genuine. It always was, in spite of the fact that this had happened other times with men who were neighbors and friends. One moment they treated me with kindness, and the next they were fondling me or kissing me passionately.

With my brother, as with these other molesters, it seemed that I had no choice but to follow my father's admonitions to be like Jesus: unselfishly meeting others' needs and showing unconditional love. Yet while one part of me believed that I was being good by showing love in these situations, I became haunted by a nagging conviction that I was a very evil person. But I couldn't let anyone know how bad I was. I couldn't let my family down, so I worked hard to bury my confused, angry feelings.

In school, even up through my high school and college years, I found some relief in reaching out to others who were suffering. I couldn't tell them of my pain and anger, but I could understand theirs. I took on the role of "savior" to my friends who were involved in alcohol, sex, and other misbehavior because they too were victims of abuse. I would do anything to prove I loved them, suffer any pain or abuse to prove that I was forgiving like Jesus. But I was always hoping that somehow, someone would find a way to love me and care enough about me to find out about my secret. But most of my friends had little to give but their hurt and anger.

After a year of college I moved to California, where I met my first husband. As usual I saw potential in him that no one else seemed to see. I believed that by loving him I could help him to forget his painful past and be happy, and that by helping him I could find happiness, too.

From the start of our marriage, I welcomed his criticism of my personal and professional life. I desperately wanted to improve, to be so good that I would be rid of that gnawing feeling that I was bad. I decided to stay at home and work harder at being what my husband needed me to be.

Soon I discovered that he was seeing other women, but when I confronted him, he explained that he needed to have many intimate relationships because of his creative work. I felt confused and guilty for being upset at him. I believed I should be an accepting and understanding wife, submissively filling all his needs, never being concerned with my own.

In my struggle with my anger I read my Bible, hoping it would help me to correct my feelings. That's what I was doing when I overheard my husband laughing on the telephone that day.

I stepped into the living room, my Bible still in hand. "I, um. I really feel . . . jealous of these women." I motioned toward the smiling photographs of his lovers he'd hung on our walls. "You talk to them all the time."

"Well," he sneered, "you know what your Bible says about jealousy. Pray about it."

And I believed him. I believed that *I* was wrong, that my feelings were evil, that they proved how selfish and bad I was. And I shut myself up in the bedroom and ached in my darkness.

Finally the sound of his footsteps invaded my silence. The door opened. "Look at you!" he gloated. "You're worthless. You're nothing. Who do you think you are?"

I looked up at him and started crying. "I love you," I sobbed. "I want you to love me, too."

"You're pitiful, and you're awful, and you need to get well. I'm moving out, but I won't divorce you because you need me." He pointed down at me and smirked, "Where's your God now?"

I felt a great painful heat rushing uncontrollably through me. Amid my emotional turmoil a tiny voice deep inside me murmured, "I'm here. I'll be with you."

For the next few weeks I couldn't stop crying. I wanted to give up and stop living. But a new career opportunity opened up, and looked at from the outside, I was a great success. As soon as I was alone I dropped my false smile and lost myself in tears or sleep.

I was torn between two desires. Some days I was relieved to be away from the abusive relationship. Other days I felt driven to pursue it with great intensity, to prove to myself that I was a good wife.

But being away from him and working on my own built my self-confidence. For a year I continued to have sexual relations with my husband on his terms, whenever he felt like it.

Time and again I felt I'd had all I could take. But every time he wanted to see me, I felt that with God's help I could erase his pain with my love. It took a long time for me to give up that hope, get a divorce, and start dating other men.

In October a friend introduced me to John. She thought we'd be a wonderful pair because he was a Christian. I wasn't sure — my first husband had said he was a Christian, too — but John and I started dating. Our relationship teetered between conflict and comradeship.

Then while I was away from John at Christmastime, I realized that my thoughts were continually turned toward him. I thought, I really like him; I respect him; he's somebody I could be friends with for a long time. Do I love him?

I'd never defined love that way. He was nothing like anyone I had ever dated before. He actually cared about me. This was a healthy Christian man, and the unknown frightened me. I struggled before finally deciding to risk marrying John rather than go back to the kind of relationships I'd always known.

My new husband treated me as I'd never been treated before. My thoughts, my ideas, and who I was were important to him. And I didn't know how to handle that. But I sought out how to please him and tried to become the perfect little wife.

When I was with him sexually, he talked to me lovingly and tried to please me as well as himself. Confusion racked my mind, and my whole body rebelled. Something inside of me couldn't handle his caresses. It didn't feel right when he was considerate of my feelings, as if I were a real person and not a thing. I expected to be treated like an object, as I always had. Tenderness and consideration were unsettling to me.

Memories of incest and abuse invaded my thoughts, and I tried to numb out, as I had then. When the terror persisted, I encouraged my husband to make love in ways that hurt me without him knowing it. At least then it seemed a little more like what I was used to.

But there were questions that refused to be silenced. I had always assured myself that those sexual intimacies had been acts of love. I had been meeting others' needs, unselfishly, unconditionally. How could that be bad? Yet if John was loving me, they hadn't loved me at all. I'd been used. But I didn't want to believe that those experiences had been abusive. It was easier to believe that my relationship with John was wrong.

I didn't make a conscious choice to withdraw from John. I was controlled by emotions erupting from within, and I couldn't talk about my feelings. I never had. Besides, I'd been trained that I must appear to others as if everything was all right.

So it was John who insisted that we go to a sex therapist because the wife who had been so open and free had turned into a cold fish. For two years we talked with the therapist about everything *but* my history of abuse. Early in our relationship I had told John about my brother, but I wasn't disturbed by it, so he felt it was all resolved. In counseling John focused on his confusion and disappointment in me, and I figured I could never please him. Both of us became more and more depressed.

I began acting the part of that evil person I believed myself to be — drinking, smoking pot, and having an affair with my ex-husband. I was back in my own familiar realm again — the realm of danger, pain, and secrets. But this didn't end my problem. Instead my self-hatred grew, and I ended up back in a closet wanting to end my life.

I decided that I needed to confess to John before I killed myself. I wanted him to understand that the things I had done weren't because of him, but because I couldn't cope with the evil in me.

We sat together on our bed, and I began trying to tell him how terrible I was.

"But you're *not* terrible. You've worked hard and done the best you could," he encouraged.

"No, no!" I screamed. "You don't understand!" The more he expressed his confidence in me, the more unworthy and evil I felt. I even began hitting and clawing at myself as I confessed my affair.

John bowed his head, silent, motionless. I watched, transfixed. He shook his head and said, "I don't know what to do. I need to think."

Later he returned. His reaction of intense anger at my ex-husband confused me. He should hate me and want me to kill myself. And he didn't. Suddenly I didn't want to kill myself anymore—because John needed me to be there for him. And I was good at that.

After a while we tried another therapist, who suggested that my problems stemmed from my sexual abuse. At this time I didn't consciously remember the other abuses, although the same nightmares kept recurring.

"But it's not a problem," I insisted. "God has already healed me." I felt talking about it would be useless. I truly believed what my church and family had taught me—that as soon as I asked, God would erase my pain and painful feelings and give me only His love and forgiveness instead.

But both the therapist and my husband seemed hopeful that I could be helped by facing this issue. And I tried to trust them.

Admitting that I felt anger, hurt, and fear was difficult for me. I struggled with the horror of facing my true emotions. I was terrified of what would happen if I brought them out and looked at them. I felt sure they would destroy me, that satan's mark would be on me forever.

My therapist, a Christian husband of an abused wife, showed great patience and empathy, both for me and my husband. For the first time in my life I began dealing with the truth of incest and abuse. Every therapy session made me shake with fear, but the sharp sense of truth struck a chord. It was playing the song of child abuse. It was a very sad song, and many times it was difficult to believe that the words *incest* and *Christian* could describe the same family. But now that the pieces began coming together, my irrational fears no longer completely controlled me. The song got easier to listen to.

John helped me through many difficult times, defending both me and himself. When I became lost in self-hatred, I ranted about how awful I was, and I blamed him, too — screaming, cursing, brutalizing my body. With calm conviction, John stood by me. He helped me see the benefit of being honest and acknowledging every emotion, but he refused to let me abuse myself or accuse him of having the same hateful feelings that I had toward myself.

Gradually John and my therapist helped me to see that all my problems didn't come from me and my choices; bad things had happened to me, and I had had nothing to do with them. As a child I had survived the best I knew how. Now I kept noticing how the abuse I had suffered had colored my life, my concept of myself. I slowly began to realize that my past doesn't have to define me and control the rest of my life.

My therapist worked at helping me to redefine words like *love* and *forgiveness*. I began to realize that God wanted me to do more than love others: it was just as important to Him that I love myself, care for and protect myself. Before I had never thought that my welfare was important. I had only taken care of others.

Now I knew that I had to do everything I could to help myself get better. During counseling memories had been revived, yet because of my dreams I believed there had been abuses I still couldn't consciously remember. Trying to put the pieces together became so frustrating that I began to question whether any of the memories were true. I decided to confront my brother. His tearful verification of my memories resolved many of my doubts. I asked my brother to give me any clues he could about others who might have abused me. In addition to suspecting some of the same men that I had remembered, he recalled being puzzled by a statement my father had made long ago about me not having a hymen. I had always wondered why my father had been in the same dreams with the others who had abused me. Together these two clues made me wonder if my father had abused me also. I decided to confront him.

Unlike my brother, my father didn't admit to abusing me. My hand tightened on the phone as he suggested one reason after another for my problems, always placing the blame on me. My body grew hot, and my heart began to race. I sat rigid on my bed facing the vanity, observing my angry reflection in the mirror.

I discovered that when I concentrated on his words, I felt like a little child again. But when I fastened my eyes on my own image, I could hold on to the reality before me. I kept thinking, Look at yourself, Sara. You're grown up, an adult with a child of your own. You're not weak, a helpless victim, out of control.

For the first time I understood what my father was doing. He was trying to get rid of life's pains, his and mine, as fast as he could. So *that* was where I'd learned to deny my feelings! Fury boiled inside me because of the damage that pattern had caused in my life.

"Honey, it doesn't matter what really happened," he continued sweetly. "God can heal you." He paused solemnly. "But I want you to know that it's very, very important that you forgive *all* the people who have harmed you, whoever they might be. And you have to forgive them right now."

"No! No, I don't!" I screamed. Thoughts of those painful hours in therapy whirled through my mind. I had worked too hard to dig up all those buried, unclaimed feelings. "Maybe I'll never know everything that happened, and maybe someday I'll forgive — but not right now."

It was the first time I had ever been strong enough to state my true emotions openly to my father without feeling I had to take care of him. I was angry because he wanted me to claim emotions that were not really mine. But I would not do it. As I stared transfixed at my livid reflection, I was surprised at how good I felt: calm, and at peace. I had been true to myself, to my own feelings, and it calmed me.

I am still working at accepting myself. I believe that God loves me, and He wants me to love myself, too. My Father in Heaven accepts me just as I am, even with my negative emotions. In fact they are His gift to me to let me know that there is something in me I need to take care of. And sometimes it's hard to be honest with myself, to love and accept myself. But acknowledging my feelings is the first step in dealing with them. And when I am honest, God can begin working in my life to bring the healing I need. And I know I can become whole through His power that strengthens me.

❧

> Father in Heaven,
> You know me completely
> and you love me.
> You can help me to know myself,
> and accept myself,
> and love myself.
> Give me courage to face my feelings
> and look beneath them
> to their source.
> I need you
> to strengthen and guide me
> as I face myself —
> my hurts,
> my feelings,
> my false beliefs.
> Thank you for hope —
> hope that helps me
> to face the truth
> so that you can set me free.
> Amen.

As we've seen in earlier chapters, many of us were living with portions of our pasts repressed. To some degree, we were living without feelings, in the numbness of chronic shock. Without a past and without feelings, there is no self. As the past two chapters delved deeper into discovering the past and discovering feelings, this one delves into discovering the self.

Dawn is a dear friend I met in a Twelve-Step group. She shares with us how she found her past, her feelings, and herself through her lost inner child.

Although the idea of the inner child was first popularized in 1963 by Hugh Missildine in Your Inner Child of the Past, *it has not reached a wide audience until now, as society has become more accepting of people dealing with the emotional pain of their childhoods.*

Numerous books are now available on the inner child concept; the best ones are listed at the back of this book. The theory is that because this is a fallen world, everyone has woundedness in their past, and therefore, a wounded inner child.

Many therapists believe that reconnecting with the lost inner child is a key part of the recovery process. I believe that the concept of the inner child is much more than a psychological tool. Jesus himself told us that unless we become like little children we cannot enter into His kingdom.

DAWN

Discovering
the Self:

The Child Within

6

Anyone who will not receive the Kingdom of God
like a little child will never enter it.   (Luke 18:17)

Hi Dawn! It's me, Dawnie. I'm happy you told me you love
me. I love you too. I've always loved you, but I never knew how
to tell you. I'm glad you let me out of the closet. It was dark,
lonely, and scary in there. I feel lost now that I'm out. Do *you*
know what to do? I guess we need each other. We need to learn
how to treat each other lovingly. Do you remember the poem
you wrote about life being like a treasure chest full of good
things but it was locked and you didn't have the key? God gave
me the key a long time ago. He knew when the time would be
right for us to unlock it. Here is the key, Dawn. I trust you with
it. I feel loved by you now. We can open the chest together.

Love,

Dawnie

❧

Dawnie is my inner child. Five years ago I didn't know she
existed. Today I have a loving and trusting relationship with
her. Reparenting her has been the key to my recovery, and

together we have opened the treasure chest of my life. What I had hoped would be gold coins, strings of pearls, diamonds, and exotic jewelry turned out to be a fire of pain and an ocean of tears. I was raised in an alcoholic home where I was raped and molested. Recovery has been difficult, but my pain and tears have been the doorway to my freedom. Today I am no longer a victim or a mere survivor. God has given me a treasure far greater than any I could have imagined. I have been set free from the corroding and sinking wreckage of my past.

I was driven toward discovery of my inner child by various symptoms. Nightmares with recurring themes plagued my sleep. The most frightening were of being engulfed and washed away by huge ocean waves, finding myself naked in a crowd of people, speeding downhill in a car without brakes, and being attacked by horrible creatures. I prayed and asked God to take away my nightmares. They only got worse.

Daytime fears paralyzed me. I was afraid to be alone, yet I had no close friends. Every time I left my house I imagined it burned to the ground by the time I returned home. Driving on the freeway would send me into a panic. Fearing that someone would crash into me and I'd be killed, I would hold my breath for too long and get sick to my stomach. I would be shaking all over by the time I exited. Paranoid about the possibility of being raped, robbed, or mugged, I had difficulty making eye contact with other people and felt intensely uncomfortable in public places. Looking back now, I realize I was unable to relax in any situation.

I prayed for God to take away my fears, but He didn't. God wanted me to discover my inner child and get her the help she deserved.

My marriage was a mess. I can remember lying face down on the floor pleading with Jesus to stop my husband from hitting my children and me. I prayed for this in secret. I didn't tell anyone about my dreams, my fears, or what was going on in my home. I suffered in silence. Wanting to tell some of the women in my Bible study group how much I was hurting in my marriage, but not able to, I asked instead for their prayers to help me be a better wife and mother.

I became obsessed with being a "perfect" Christian, which made my walk with the Lord feel like a boat ride in stormy seas. Inside I felt tossed and tumbled in deep waters of doubt, confusion, and shame. I doubted God's love for me. I was convinced I wasn't as good as the other Christians at church. On the outside I tried my best to earn God's love and approval. I covered my inner feeling of absolute inadequacy by going to church every week, reading my Bible daily, and attending a weekly women's Bible study group.

No matter how hard I tried, though, I could not fill the emptiness inside me. I worked hard for God, but I still felt lost in a fog, alone and drifting with no place to call my own. I felt different from everyone else. It was an ache that no amount of "Christianese" could take away. Sitting in church was extremely uncomfortable for me because the music and sermons brought waves of tears to my eyes. I had to fight them back; I was ashamed to cry in church. To me, tears meant I wasn't okay. I didn't know God wanted to heal me through my tears; I didn't know that to Him my tears were beautiful. It was easier for me to help out in Sunday school or the nursery than to be embarrassed by my tears in the worship service. I saw other people cry in church, but they were surrounded by friends who offered them comfort. I didn't have any close friends in church. I realize now that was because I hadn't reached out.

What I didn't realize was that my view of God was distorted because the father figures in my early childhood had abandoned, abused, and raped me. Whenever songs about God the Father were sung in church, my chest would tighten and tears would come. If I let God into the deepest part of my heart, would He leave me? If I trusted Him to be my Father, would He hurt me? I wasn't ready to let God get this close — at least not yet.

As I made a commitment to try to show up regularly to my Bible study group, I began to make friends with a few of the women there. Finally, after one year, I heard myself say during prayer time, "My husband hits me when he's angry."

Vicki, a friend who had shared that her father had molested her as a child, said to me, "Dawn, you are a battered wife. He abuses you."

Her words rang in my ears. I thought to myself, Me? Abused? Battered? Out loud I questioned, "I am?"

"Yes, you are," Vicki answered softly.

Tears welled in my eyes and began to trickle down my cheeks. I knew she was right, but I didn't want to admit the truth. I hung my head and prayed. In my mind, God showed me a picture of a door. I thought it was another room God was going to lead me into the way He had so many times before. I labeled it my "room of abuse" and prayed for my husband to stop battering me. He didn't. God spent another year gently preparing me for the day I would open this door. How this happened is an example of God's perfect timing — and His sense of humor.

God's surprise came disguised as my attempt to rescue a neighbor of mine, Joe, a man in his seventies who had a drinking problem. I waited patiently for the day he told me he was ready for help. Knowing what to do, I jumped at the chance to "save" him. I drove him to a Twelve-Step group at my church for Christians struggling with chemical dependency. With a smile on my face and cradling my youngest son in my arms, I arrived — the picture-perfect image of an angelic rescuer. A sense of pride swept over me, and I stayed with Joe for the duration of the meeting, thinking my presence would provide him a familiar face of security. Ironically, I was the one who needed help from this group!

God is so clever! He knew the only way I would make it to a meeting like this was to bring in a needy friend. "Keep coming back, it works," was spoken out loud in unison at the end of the meeting. My hands were squeezed, and I was warmly hugged by several people. Feeling confused, I stood in shock. Why did being hugged feel so good and so bad at the same time? What was I doing in this room of recovering alcoholics, addicts, spouses of alcoholics, and grown children of alcoholic parents? God knew the reason. I remained ignorant.

I did keep coming back. It started working. Through the hearts of caring people in the meetings, God created a safe harbor for me to share my deepest pain. After four months, I gained the strength and growth I needed to confront my husband with his physical battering of my children and me. I filed a suspected child abuse report with the aid of one of the pastors at my church, and court proceedings followed. My four children were made wards of the court for six months while my husband and I entered individual counseling and attended parenting classes.

In therapy, I realized I had grown up in a dysfunctional home. My mother and step-father were alcoholics. It would take me a year to be able to admit this. I also began having blocked memories return. One by one, memories returned of having been molested by strangers, friends of family members, and even family members. The molestation I remembered first happened when I was seven. Later I remembered incidents at the ages of five, twelve, fifteen, and seventeen.

In addition to therapy I began to attend a support group for incest victims and a Twelve-Step self-help group for adults who were raised in alcoholic homes.

While I was praying and meditating with God, the painful but wonderful day arrived. Once again a flash of a closet door showed up on the screen of my mind. I knew God wanted me to open it. Reluctantly, I placed my hand on the doorknob. Scared of what I might see, I closed my eyes and nervously pulled the door open about four inches. I looked in. It was dark, and I could barely see the small figure hovering in the corner. I asked God if I could do this some other time; I didn't feel ready. But the room lit up just enough for me to see her. I shuddered. Standing before me was a frightened little girl no more than seven years old. Her sad eyes stared back at me from out of a dirty, tear-stained face. Cold, wet, and shivering, she was scrawny and looked as if she hadn't eaten for days.

I wanted to slam the door shut and never open it again, but God helped me keep it open. In His loving and gentle, but persistent way, He told me if I closed the door now it would be like suicide. The terrified little girl was me. She was who I am on the inside. Now I understood. God was trying to tell me I had been abused as a child, even though it was hard for me to believe. My heart had been pierced by the deep sadness of this little girl I called Dawnie. I didn't entirely understand why she was so sad, but I told her I loved her and asked her if I could hug her. She nodded her head up and down. I walked over to her and tenderly wrapped my arms around her. I began to cry. I cried so loud and so hard that my lungs, ribs, and stomach hurt. I grabbed my pillow and rocked myself between sobs.

Somehow I knew these tears were different. They belonged to Dawnie. I had kept them in for a very long time. She was me. I held her and let her cry. It was my first lesson in reparenting. I told her it was okay to cry and promised I would help her and love her. She knew I would not put her back in the closet. For the very first time in eight years of being a Christian, I *felt* God's love for me in my heart. Now I understood what He was talking about when He told me to love my neighbor as myself. Showing love to Dawnie like this was being able to receive God's love for me. Only now could I truly show love to others.

Over the next months, God proceeded to teach me how to have conversations with Dawnie. I learned how to keep a journal and to communicate with her through writing. I wrote questions to her using my right hand and let her answer using my left hand (because I am right-handed). I discovered my real needs were the same as my inner child's. I had to start over and reparent her with healthy messages she had never received as a child. One big breakthrough in getting to know God as my perfect Father was when I learned it was okay to get mad at God. Today when I feel angry I go straight to God and dump on Him. Then I share it with a friend. That way I don't end up taking it out on the innocent ones around me.

I had been abusive to my children. I overreacted to normal childhood mistakes. I would make intimidating threats and give unnecessary spankings. Essentially, I took my frustrations out on my children, blaming them for a situation that was not their fault.

In February of 1988, after three and a half years of therapy and support groups, Dawnie felt safe enough to reveal to me what had happened to me when I was three years old. It took me another year and a half of single flashbacks to put all the pieces together. In the arms of a close friend I told the story as if it were rolling on film before my eyes.

It was late at night. I woke up and had to go to the bathroom. Normally, my sister would help me turn on the bathroom light. On this night she was away, perhaps sleeping over at a friend's house. Being only three, I couldn't reach the light switch, so I started jumping, hoping I could somehow flick it on in the middle of one of my jumps.

Suddenly I heard footsteps. They were loud, hard, and fast. I felt my chest tighten, and my heart started to pound faster. The footsteps stopped and the light went on. A tall man was standing before me with a yellow towel wrapped around his waist. His eyes were flashing with anger, and I felt a lump in my throat as he stared at me. Without warning, he took off his towel and roughly anchored his hand behind my head. He gripped me with such force that I was sure he would kill me. He took his other hand and squeezed my jawbones to force his penis in my mouth. I was suffocating. I don't remember how long it took him to ejaculate, but I remember him laughing and saying, "Your mother does a good job." I felt like I had to throw up from being forced to swallow. My throat was on fire.

Evidently I had interrupted him and my mother in her bedroom (he was my mother's boyfriend in between her divorce and remarriage), and he was angry about having to get up and help me. The smell of alcohol was heavy on his breath. It felt as though his penis was crammed in my mouth forever, and I couldn't breathe. Then he was gone. The most humiliating part of the experience for my three-year-old self was looking down at my legs afterward and discovering I had urinated all over myself and was standing in a huge puddle of it. In a frenzy I rushed to clean it up before the "monster" came back to get me.

My sister was always like a mother to me; she always took care of me at night. But she wasn't there. I was too scared to cry. I was too scared to make a noise of any kind. All I could think of to do was ask the dark to be my friend. I went back into my room, crawled into my bed, and draped the sheet up over my nose, leaving just my eyes and forehead uncovered. I was in shock, and I had no one to take care of me.

In the morning I had to eat breakfast with this man. I just sat there staring at my bowl of cereal. I couldn't eat. I couldn't tell anyone because I was afraid he would kill me if I told. I was too scared to tell my mother. I was afraid she would punish me for lying. From that moment on, Dawnie blocked the memory for me. She was a survivor.

My friend held me as I spoke and choked on my tears. I cried for days after that and went into a kind of shock for several weeks. I retold my story as many times as I could in my meetings within those first few weeks. Each time I shared what had happened to me it was less painful to talk about. I still cry when I share what happened to little Dawnie, but the gut-wrenching, chest-heaving sobs are gone.

Gone too is the power this man had over me for so many years. No longer am I terrified of men, especially tall ones. My night terrors have been laid to rest. I still have bad dreams during times of stress, but they are mild compared to the nightmares I used to have. My daytime fears have diminished so much that I actually enjoy driving on the freeway, and I now feel confident in a crowd of people even if it's in a place I've never been before. I can relax more easily today and no longer suffer from anorexia and asthma. I can cry in front of others and not feel ashamed. I don't have to be a perfect Christian anymore; I know God loves me just the way I am. I am able to show anger toward God without fear of losing my relationship with Him. I have developed a sense of belonging in my small circle of close friends and my support group network.

I am divorced from my husband, but I don't consider myself a failure as a wife. I understand now why I chose to marry him; it was Dawnie's way of trying to tell me what happened to her. I have learned that I do not have to stay in an abusive situation, whether it's physical or mental. I am beginning to feel pretty, intelligent, capable, and lovable after over thirty years of feeling ugly, stupid, inadequate, and unlovable.

Today I face difficulties without using symptomatic behavior to bury my feelings. Dawnie helps me stay in touch with my feelings, and I understand now that they are given by God to help me chart my adventures in living one day at a time. I can take risks, hug other people and receive hugs, laugh, cry, celebrate life, talk about feelings, grieve and offer comfort to others. God has restored the years the locust had eaten. My life is living proof. Today, Dawnie knows God as her Daddy. He is seared in her heart, and she knows He will always love her and never abandon her, no matter what.

๛

Hi Daddy God, it's me, Dawnie. I love you. I'm glad you love me. I need you to hold me because I have to cry, Daddy.

I was angry at you yesterday because I was hurt and scared. No one seems to care about me. It feels like I'm all alone and there isn't anyone to make me feel better. I'm afraid I am going to die if I have to feel this pain anymore. I didn't want to get mad at everybody else so I got mad at you instead.

I'm sorry I called you all those bad names. Please forgive me. You don't hit me, choke me, and say "I'm going to kill you" when I get angry. I don't have to hide in my closet and cry because you don't call me a crybaby. You forgive me. You tell me I can get mad at you and you will understand. You love me no matter what. Thank you for loving and hugging me.

I love you, Jesus. I like it when you hold me softly in your strong arms. It makes me feel safe. Sometimes Dawn forgets you are here. She doesn't like to cry. I do. It takes the ouchie out of my heart when I cry. You have bottles full of my tears you are keeping for me. I don't feel alone anymore, Daddy. I feel you are right here, face to face, heart to heart.

I love you forever,

Dawnie

Growing
Toward the
Light

Each person who has been involved in this journey of healing has become a friend. What a blessing it has been for me to meet my friend De Ette!

I would never have known her before, not only because our backgrounds are so different, but because my own sins of judgmentalism and self-righteousness would have gotten in the way.

Little Miss Perfect Christian, I might have thought to myself, Why, I can't associate with her; what would people think?

Like me, De Ette was sexually abused as a child. Like me, she tried to ease her pain. I eased my pain with workaholism, excessive volunteerism, self-righteousness, a critical spirit, judgmentalism, and other things I am not yet ready to share — I'm not yet as honest as De Ette is.

De Ette eased her pain with heroin, which led her into prostitution and the loss of three addicted babies. Her daughters were taken away from her. She is God's precious child, and my sister.

In her story, De Ette shares with us how God is setting her free from the bondage of her past, as she grows closer to Jesus — toward the Light.

D E E T T E

Recovering
the Past

7

Humble yourselves before the Lord, and he will lift
you up. (James 4:10)

I jumped at the sound of pounding on the door downstairs. I could tell the person wouldn't give up until he had
what he wanted. Albert, the man I was living with, sensed it,
too. He frowned, withdrawing the needle from where he was
tattooing my leg. "Get it," he muttered.

Obediently I hurried down the narrow stairs. Maybe it was
some desperate friend of Albert's wanting drugs or protection.
Maybe it was the police coming after Albert or me.

I opened the door, certain the noise would end. How
wrong could I be? In the doorway stood my mother, her eyes
bulging with rage. My heart pounding, I turned to run out the
other door. My mother's screams engulfed me.

"I'm going to get you! Why do you want to hang around
these losers? If you're pregnant, you're getting an abortion!"

My stomach twisted into a sick knot. I yanked the other
door open, only to find my sister blocking my way. She grabbed
my arm. Then my mother snatched me by the hair and began
dragging me out the door.

I could have resisted, but I was so humiliated by her screaming that I stumbled along, hoping she'd stop before everyone in the housing project witnessed my shame.

Finally we reached our house, and Mother released her grip. I discovered that my girlfriend, also thirteen years old, had told her where I was because she was upset with me. After my mother vented her anger, she took a deep breath and motioned toward the couch. We settled down for a smoke as if nothing had happened. Why didn't she ask what had happened to me while I was away for two whole months? Or even why I'd run away from home?

I rubbed my sore scalp, trying to understand my own feelings. In spite of my problems at home, I felt a strange sense of relief, as if I'd been rescued. My freedom from home had had its price.

Albert, my twenty-year-old boyfriend, became violent easily, especially when drunk. Without warning he would beat me in a jealous rage. And night after night he awakened me demanding that I satisfy his unending appetite for sex. I had to please him if I wanted food, shelter, and drugs.

I sighed, thinking of what I had returned to. We'd moved in with my aunt and uncle four years ago, when I was nine, after my parents' divorce. Mom and my aunt worked nights, and I cared for the house and my brother and three sisters. I really didn't mind. But it seemed that I was always taking care of someone else, and no one was taking care of me.

But maybe I wasn't worth caring about. Three months after we moved in, my uncle began molesting me. My eyes would blink with sleep as he led me by the hand to his bed. Shame was mixed with puzzling emotions and delightful sensations. How could I feel so good when I knew what we did was bad? I must be bad, very bad, or I wouldn't have these feelings. I didn't even think of telling anyone; I couldn't talk about ordinary feelings, let alone something as perplexing as this.

In seventh grade, I'd begun cutting school with two of my girlfriends because I needed to do something just for myself. We went to the tracks where older gang members hung out. We looked up to them as our role models. They did drugs and served time in jail; we wanted to be just like them.

At thirteen I began trying drugs — acid and reds — out of curiosity. They made me feel happy and let me escape from my uneasiness about myself and my life.

For a long time Mom didn't know I cut school. When she found out that I wasn't living up to her expectations, things got worse. She yelled and called me names. I never argued or tried to explain how I felt. How could I? She was so much smarter than I, and her life was difficult enough already. She'd lost my father; she worked nights and studied days; she really wanted to make something of herself — and me. I felt sorry that I couldn't please her.

From her point of view, she did everything a mother needed to do: she provided us with food and shelter. I wished that I could have been happy with that, but I wanted to be loved, and she never knew how to communicate love the way I needed it. So I searched for love in the arms of men and ran away from home when I couldn't take hearing her yell about how I'd disappointed her.

For a month after my mother dragged me away from Albert, I tried — I really tried — to stick with school. But the other young people were too different. They hadn't experienced what I had, and I knew I didn't belong. I had to go where I could be accepted for who I was.

During my early teen years I ran away many times. I walked unfamiliar streets, away from my gang, and no one looked after me there. I danced, had sex, drank, and did drugs, making myself vulnerable to an uncaring world. I was raped many times, most often when I was numb on dope. Strangely enough, those times didn't haunt me as much as my earlier abuse by my uncle—perhaps because these were strangers, and by now I'd already decided I wasn't worthy of much respect anyhow.

On two traumatic occasions I was tied to a bed and raped repeatedly for three days before being released. While lying helpless and fully aware of my abuse, I nursed a growing hatred for men. I vowed that when I got away, I would do everything in my power to hurt every man I could.

When I was fifteen, I found a boyfriend who was a true companion. We had fun partying together, and we could communicate. I trusted him and wanted to be a good woman for him. At seventeen I gave birth to his child. But when our son was six months old, my boyfriend died of a heroin overdose.

I was devastated—aching with grief over losing the one man I loved. When one of his friends told me that I would feel better if I used heroin, I felt I had no choice. Day after day I survived my pain with an injection.

My grief consumed me. I could think of nothing else, not even my young son. I left him in my mother's care, and continued to run from my pain.

To get drugs I needed money, but I refused to lower myself to prostitution. I had sex with any man I wanted: after all, wasn't that the purpose of my body—to bring pleasure to others? Yet giving myself for pay was beneath me. Prostitution and homosexuality were two things I refused to have anything to do with. So I began stealing, and that wasn't hard, because I had often shoplifted pretty things we couldn't afford. But now that I stole so much, I sometimes got caught and ended up in jail at least a dozen times.

I lived this way for five years, trying to survive, just survive, and not be overwhelmed with guilt, pain, and loneliness.

During this period I tried religion, too. We had attended
church before my mother gave up on my father and left him,
and I had always believed that God was important. But now
even though I envied the change I saw God make in some of
my addict friends, I just couldn't trust God completely. I wasn't
sure that He'd really be able to satisfy my needs. I'd always
survived and gained respect by never showing softness, so I
refused to make a decision for Christ. And from that point on I
went down — down farther than I ever thought I could go.

One morning in jail after doing night duty in the kitchen,
I lay back on my bunk for a smoke before going to sleep.

"Your time's about up, isn't it?" asked the blonde on the
next cot.

"Only two weeks."

"What'd you get busted for?"

"Burglary."

She shook her head. "Why should you bother with such
high-risk crime? You've got the looks for being a great call girl."
She gave me an approving gaze as she drew on her cigarette.
"You could be making a thousand dollars a trick and getting
cars, clothes, and expensive gifts. You'd go to the best restau-
rants and hotels. They're nice men — judges, lawyers, doctors.
They won't hurt you; they just need an attractive woman."

I thought about all the times I'd been busted in my five
years of addiction. And what she said made sense. Besides,
from the first time my uncle used me, I sensed that I was meant
for that kind of life anyway.

"Here," she said, handing me a paper with a name and
phone number. "Get smart, De Ette, and when you get out, call
my madame and she'll set you up real nice."

I tucked the paper in my locker. By the time I got out, I'd
decided that I had no other choice if I wanted to stay out of jail.

To survive prostitution and be good at it, I had to numb my shame and hatred with drugs. Finally, having drugs became more important to me than pleasing my clients, and I kept feeling worse and worse about myself—and them. They didn't love me or fulfill me sexually. They only wanted me to please them, and my hatred for men grew.

I masturbated to try to satisfy my own need for love. With sadomasochism I vented my rage against men and got paid big bucks for it. But it was the same story. Every time I had all the luxuries I could dream of and the possibility of more and more, I ruined it all by running off to make a drug pick up. The turmoil of hatred of myself and others drove me in search of relief. But nothing satisfied my desire to be loved.

Finally, in spite of my abhorrence of homosexuality, I became involved several times in jail, hoping that I'd find the love I craved. And I did experience gentleness, something different than with the men I'd been with, but I paid for it with a further loss of self-esteem.

While in jail I became involved with the woman I would live with for five years. Even though she didn't do drugs, she loved me, communicated with me, took care of me, accepted me and my drug habit. She stuck with me when I was in and out of jail, when I prostituted for drug money, and when I had a baby girl. As with two other addicted daughters, I gave the baby away right after birth. Gradually my world started closing in on me. I had no future, no hope. I wanted to die. Many nights when I was in jail, I cried out to God from my bunk in solitary confinement. I knew He was real, and I wanted to know Him, but I didn't know if He could really help me.

I began to sense God's hand at work in my life. But it didn't really make sense. Why did He protect me from the maniac tricks who had killed three of my friends recently? Why didn't He let me die when I twice overdosed on drugs and, both times, was mistaken for dead by paramedics?

Even these events couldn't wake me up. I was burned out. I got sick of my lover and told her to get out. I was running from the cops. My arms were so bad that even after I worked to hustle up enough money for a good fix, I didn't have any-place to shoot up. My arms and neck were useless and puss-covered. Frustration and fear racked my shaking body. How could I survive? How could I die?

Then my sister's seven-year-old daughter was killed by a reckless driver. How could God be so unfair? Why had He taken an innocent little child and let someone as terrible as me go on living?

I watched my sister's reaction to her tragedy with amaze-ment. Earlier, she had accepted Christ, and now I witnessed her pain and how she clung to God and His promises for her strength.

During the days I spent with my sister, I saw many of the people who had used drugs with me and had been in jail with me. As I watched my sister and my friends who had turned to Jesus, I could hardly believe the changes I saw. Maybe God had enough power, maybe He had enough love, to help me, too.

I had nothing to lose. Drugs couldn't do me any good. My hatred of men consumed me. My son lived with his grandpar-ents and my three daughters had been adopted by friends. I didn't see them. I realized that my children were with people who were better able to care for them than I was. As sad as I was to realize my children didn't need me, I began to think of rehabilitation.

Within three days after my niece's funeral, I'd turned my life over to God, gotten rid of all my belongings, and checked in to Victory Outreach Rehabilitation Home for help.

This decisive action released a torrent of raging guilt. Could God love me? I felt so cheap and ugly. Memories flashed through my mind: my abortions, my three daughters, my ne-glected son, the men I'd hated and exploited, every perverted thing I'd done. I couldn't hold back the hatred I'd had all these years for myself and my body. I felt sick with shame. Could God really love and forgive me?

I determined that I'd give God a try. I knew in my heart that if I didn't find peace in His love, I'd return to the streets, die in my sin, and go to hell. This was my last chance.

I faced my withdrawal from heroin with grim determination. Although I was kicking with the agony of withdrawal, I asked for chores to do around the home — at least that way I could keep my mind on something other than my cravings. In the first two weeks God freed me of my desire for heroin, cigarettes, and drinking.

I still agonized over my desire for my lover. I was brokenhearted, because I knew that if I was to have a real relationship with God, I'd have to give her up. She had been more than a lover; she was my best friend and my family as well. She met my needs as no one had ever done. She took care of me, loved me, welcomed me back with open arms when I'd run away to hustle and get a fix. Who would I have, if I didn't have her? Could God give me a life in which I could love and be loved in return?

As I confessed my needs and fears to God in prayer, God met me and made Himself known to me in a beautiful way. He assured me that He could fill the emptiness of my life and mend my broken heart.

And He did.

This healing didn't take place all at once, but God showed me that I am important to Him and that He can use me to minister to others as well. For six years God has kept me clean and helped me to grow closer to Him through His word and prayer. He continues to heal, restore, and bless my life far beyond what I could hope for. He strengthens me in the difficult times and directs my life. He often gives me the opportunity of working with others who have had problems similar to mine.

When I walked into Newberry's one day not long ago, I noticed a very thin girl shoplifting jewelry. Immediately I knew that she was into drugs. She reminded me so much of myself! I walked over to her and noticed she was fingering some earrings in the shape of a cross.

"Jesus died for you on the cross," I said. "He knows what you're going through, and He loves you."

She gazed at me with watery eyes. I saw her pain and anguish, the tracks of needle marks on her arms.

"I know you don't love yourself, but Jesus loves you. I didn't love myself either. I didn't think I was worth loving. But then I got to know Jesus. And I learned that I am precious in His eyes. God has healed my broken heart and given me back what I lost. He helped me learn to love myself."

"I really needed to hear that," she whispered. "I'm dying of AIDS." I wasn't surprised. Sores covered her body, and she looked awful. "I'd like to know more. Would you give me your phone number?"

As I watched her walk away, I prayed that she would be able to believe in God's love and turn to Him for healing, forgiveness, and newness of life. "He who conceals his sins does not prosper, but whoever confesses and renounces them finds mercy" (Prov. 28:13).

ࢯ

Dear Jesus,
Thank you
for loving me when I felt no one else did,

for reaching out to me in my pain,
for healing my broken heart.
Thank you
for forgiving me
for all the terrible things I have done,
and for helping me to forgive others
who sinned against me.
I didn't think anyone could love me as you do.
I didn't think I'd ever be able to love myself.
But your love and power to restore
are beyond comprehension.
Continue to heal my inner child
and teach me how to love and trust.
I give you my life.
Amen.

In De Ette's chapter, we saw how our heavenly Father is redeeming her past. Because of her willingness to be open, He is using her in a powerful way.

In her chapter, Emma will focus on how the Lord is helping her to recover her feelings. As painful as this process is, it is what stops the abuse from passing on to another generation. The Lord is giving Emma the courage she needs to go through the pain so she can protect her own children.

Now is a good time to point out that the recovery process is different for each individual. The arrangement of chapters around the framework of uncovering, discovering, and recovering, is an attempt to give a sense of order to a process that is unique to each person. Each contributor has written about only a portion of her or his process.

Emma is my sister in the Lord and also, like Dan in Chapter 3, she is part of my family of recovery.

EMMA

Recovering the Feelings

8

Fear not for I have redeemed you; I have summoned you by name, you are mine. When you pass through the waters I will be with you; and when you pass through the rivers, they will not sweep over you. When you walk through the fire you will not be burned; the flames will not set you ablaze.
(Isaiah 43:1–2)

The clock on the nightstand said 5:45 A.M. My eyes closed as my mind began to think back over the past month. Today was my last day at the hospital. The thought left me feeling sad; it was funny I'd feel sad. Just a few months back I was so adamant against "needing" to check in as a patient, to work through my incest issues.

After all, it wasn't as if I'd grown up not knowing I'd been molested when I was thirteen and fourteen. My mother's boyfriend, or "Daddy," as I referred to him for so many years, was even out of my life now. I had been working off and on for the past seven years on the effect the abuse had had on my life.

It had been only a year ago when I decided to get into counseling again. I was determined this time to finish this "incest business" once and for all and get on with my life. I remember praying and asking the Lord for a good counselor. I was tired of thinking about what had happened to me. I didn't identify myself as a victim anymore. I wasn't about to drag my recovery out forever. I didn't intend to spend the rest of my life in counseling and support groups. At age thirty, I had better things to do with my time.

I had even meant it when I told the Lord, "I'll face anything in my past, as long as you face it with me." Little did I know then the memories I'd selectively erased from my mind years before. I had been able to destroy the mental photographs that were too painful to remember. I only left those snapshots of my dad that fit the happy family image. But God knew the pain of the little girl I had been and who was still inside me and knew about my attempts to destroy her over the years. He knew soon I'd be willing to face the part of myself I despised most, that little girl who stood as a constant reminder of everything I had vowed I wouldn't become. She was that part of myself that was once vulnerable, frightened, and powerless, unable to protect herself against being hurt. "A victim, a spineless wimp," I had once called her.

I'd assumed I'd grown up in an average home, that my childhood had been normal until I was molested at thirteen. Over the years the truth began to trickle out slowly. My daddy wasn't really my daddy, nor was he married to my mother. He was married to another woman. His sons were his "real" children. Still, he was the closest thing I had to a real daddy. At the age of two I emotionally adopted him as my father. That's who he remained for the next twenty-four years—my daddy. I adored him.

I had gradually built an illusion of what our family was. It became the only truth I knew. I thought that someday Mom and Dad would get married; then we would do all the things other families did. We would go camping, take vacations together, and Mom and Dad would love each other. More important, my sister and I would have a daddy to love and care for us.

The years wore on, and my fantasy day never arrived. My sister married and started her own family. I entered my teens. It was then that life began to give way beneath me.

It seemed as if I went from playing with Ken and Barbie dolls to being Daddy's private playmate. My first memories of my father's sexual advances center on when I was thirteen. My mother would leave for work in the morning, and my father would come into my room. I remember many mornings of waking up to my father's hands fondling me beneath my clothes. I tried to lie still and pretend I was asleep, avoiding any direct acknowledgment of this intrusion.

The pain of the truth became too great to bear. At thirteen I began to find temporary relief in drugs and alcohol. Life began to lose its meaning and worth, and I lashed out in all directions. I would eventually be caught stealing, only to continue. Missing school became commonplace, often with Dad's consent. I was failing miserably in school and began thinking of ways to end my life. The numbing effects of increased use of drugs and alcohol distanced me from reality, but they allowed me to exist for the time being. My dad became a target for my rage.

By the time I began high school, the abuse had ended. Life gradually began to stabilize. In college I discovered meaning and direction in my newfound belief and relationship in Jesus Christ. The years that followed were filled with life's joys and struggles.

By the time my husband and I celebrated our eleventh anniversary God had blessed us with two wonderful daughters. We held a Bible study/support group in our home for several years. It was during one of those meetings that the stark reality of my childhood came crashing in, without warning or need for approval. The scene that followed was so removed from my life that I looked on without much emotion. It was as if I were viewing a movie on a screen.

Depicted before me was a man tying down a woman, then raping her and placing objects into her. A look of terror filled her face. I could hear her cries for help through her gagged mouth.

I wasn't sure what any of this meant or how it was connected to me. I especially didn't understand why the man seemed to be my dad and the woman myself. Surely, I thought, I'd have some recollection of it if such an incident were part of my past.

When I spoke with my counselor about it he told me that what I had seen could be literal or symbolic. If it was an actual event, additional memories would surface. Whether or not the memories were literal, the feelings were what was important to focus on.

By now I had begun to fear the worst. Maybe there was some truth in this mental picture. Hearing my counselor suggest that I focus on the feelings rather than the memory was a relief. This would be easy and nonthreatening. I was accustomed to writing my thoughts in my journal. I began the task later that afternoon but was hardly prepared for the sequence of physical and mental flashbacks I'd tapped into.

As I wrote, my mind vividly confirmed what I had seen the day before. My memory banks exposed even more of the raw truth that had been locked away. As much as my mind wanted to deny what it saw, it couldn't refute my body's recollections. It became increasingly difficult to breathe. Soon it felt as if something heavy weighted down my chest. My arms felt as if they were pinned down, and I wanted to throw up. I saw my father sitting on my chest, forcing me to engage in oral sex.

The dam of denial had broken. I could no longer pretend I was not connected with the information. Everything within me screamed in confirmation of this suppressed nightmare.

As time went on I gained more information about this man that I called Daddy. He was violent, cruel, and sadistic. My mind had separated the two sides of him. The little girl within me said, "No, that's not my daddy. My daddy wouldn't do those things to me. My daddy loves me. That other man is a stranger; I don't know him."

The denial continued breaking down, and I seemed to be in shock much of the time. The knowledge of the extent of my abuse overwhelmed me. There were days when I grieved and cried for that abused child. There were other days when I doubted everything I knew and felt that these things could *not* have happened to me. It was as if I had awakened one day and begun living someone else's nightmare.

The memories indicated I had been much younger than thirteen when I was first abused. The ages in my flashbacks kept getting earlier and earlier. Finally the images settled at between two and three years of age, with the abuse ending at fourteen. My memories now included being photographed, tied down, tortured, and threatened with death if I told anyone.

Although my subconscious seemed relieved at letting go of the buried, infected wounds, my conscious mind began feeling desperate. The desire to live disappeared. I told God one night that I couldn't continue living as I was. I ask Him to either give me a purpose for life or let me die and be with Him.

My counselor had suggested for the second or third time that I enter a hospital program. There I could process my information and emotions in a safe, supportive environment.

My world seemed to be falling apart. I would burst into tears at any moment; I couldn't concentrate at work and I had to drop the college classes I was enrolled in. My frantic attempts to hold it together failed. I finally came to the end of myself. I knew I needed a safe environment so I could begin letting down the protective barriers I had erected in childhood that were now roadblocks in my life.

One of my fears about going into the program was that I would come out just knowing better how to survive. I was so tired and worn out; I needed more than just good tools to use. I told God I had to have a reason to go on. I wanted hope for the future, something to live for.

Although I was surrounded by people who loved me and had many other good things in my life, these external things and relationships were no longer enough. I knew that people or programs could not give me what I so desperately wanted. I was in a scary place, feeling like someone in limbo.

While in the hospital I got further in touch with my memories. Daily group sessions, role play in psychodrama, and sodium amytal (used to lower natural defences) interviews helped me to connect with the feelings and emotions I had repressed for years.

God began to introduce me to the little girl I had once been, the one He had created. It was this little girl who loved her daddy. It was that very love that her daddy used against her to physically, mentally, and emotionally overpower her. She was not worthless and didn't deserve to be treated in such a degrading way, but he had taken her natural innocence, twisted the truth, and betrayed her.

I saw a child who had endured abuse and torture beyond my understanding. In spite of it, she had fought for her life. I saw a courageous little girl who had a strong desire to go on. This surprised me, because I did not feel that way as an adult.

This was not the little girl I had previously perceived. I had thought she was a child so emotionally beaten down that she was beyond hope. Since I couldn't get rid of her I resented her; as long as she remained vulnerable and powerless I could still be victimized.

I had much to learn from this child whom I had deserted years ago. I felt as if God had literally opened a window inside of me and introduced me to the child *He* knew and created.

I truly believe He began to give me back to myself during that period. My mind returned to the present as I thought of a quote hanging in one of the hospital offices. It had been an anchor to me when I wondered if anything within me would remain. Martin Luther King expressed it so beautifully when he said, "I have held many things and lost them. . . . But whatever I have placed in God's hand I still possess."

I thought of what lay ahead of me as I prepared to return home. I knew that in many ways the work had just begun; I was still in the process of uncovering more memories. I also had to learn to connect the memories with the actual feelings.

With much difficulty I began looking at my family more realistically. My stomach became uneasy as I recalled past discussions with my mother, older sister, and aunt.

When I first began disclosing my sexual abuse by my father, seven years ago, my mother wanted to know why I had not gone to her for help and protection. At that time, he was out of our lives forever. She informed me she would have incarcerated her lover at once if she had only known.

My older sister Tina, later echoed similar sentiments, then asked why I had protected my father for so long and stated she would never have done such a thing. My aunt also stated how she wished she would have known about the abuse in order to do something. My mother, sister, and aunt reassured me of their concern for my well being.

As the intensity of my abuse unraveled before me so did their lack of support. It was during my last days at the hospital when I began to realize my brother-in-law's overtures toward me as a girl were in fact inappropriate and abusive. As a teen he had shown me pornographic material and had spoken of acts of beastiality. I had carried the guilt and shame and assumed I had somehow brought this on myself. It was only recently that I understood the residue of my brother-in-law's emotional and sexual abuse was no longer mine to carry or conceal.

I made the decision to confront my brother-in-law in the next few months. When I spoke to my mother about my decision, she reacted in anger and hostility, stating I was purposely ruining my sister's marriage over nothing at all. She charged that if I continued saying such awful things, she might die of a heart attack or go insane.

I was also met with a great deal of denial and anger from my sister. I was hurt and taken aback by her hostility and lack of understanding.

My mother specifically asked that I'd promise not to say anything that would upset anyone. My sister and aunt in turn told me not to upset my mother.

These significant women in my family reassured me again of their love. Simultaneously, they requested I not betray the unspoken oath of silence that still controlled their lives.

I was aware of what I would be facing. I realized the outcome might be rejection and isolation from these and possibly other relatives.

The adults protected the adults. They said nothing of the possibility that their own children might also have been molested or approached sexually by these two men. They could sacrifice the truth even though their own children might pay the cost of that sacrifice.

I think that God must look down from heaven and cry for the children who are victims of silence, sacrificed needlessly by the very people who should love and protect them.

When I told my mother I would not lie to cover up for others, she said, "You don't have to lie. Just don't say anything." Her words made me know that I would have to risk losing her approval and that of my other family members. Coming out of hiding and beginning to walk in the new truth I was learning would be an important part of my healing.

I have to remind myself on my hard days when I feel fearful, disillusioned, or distant from God that the cycle of abuse is, in fact, being broken. I look at the continual changes in my own life and the open doors with my children and other children in the family, and I slowly understand why it is worth facing the opposition from others — it is making a difference in my life and theirs.

As I continue to speak more openly, I realize that bridges of communication to the children are being built. When I share with them and answer questions I am giving them a safe person to turn to and permission to speak.

I've come to know and trust that the God who walked through my past with me will continue to take my hand and walk through the present and future with me also.

೭ॐ

Dear Lord,
How do I put into words
what seems like years of pain and hurt?
The words are either vague and distant,
or harsh and exposing.
My mind screams in denial at the impact of their meaning
and the connection with someone known,
let alone myself.

The words are inadequate to describe
the loss I feel inside.
And yet, it's these very words
that break years of lies and deceptions
and give way to hope
making new life possible.

But, the death of denial is
such a harsh reality.

Still,
words are inadequate to describe
the loss I feel inside

Thank you, Lord, for the words you've given me.

"I will give you the treasures of darkness, riches stored
in secret places, so that you may know that I am the
Lord, the God of Israel, who summons you by name."
(Isa. 45:3)

The earlier sections, surviving the darkness and struggling out of the darkness, dealt only with the self. In this section,
however, growing toward the light, we begin to look at intimacy with others.

In this next chapter, Gregory shares himself with us. His
willingness to be vulnerable, transparent, and used by God has
been a blessing to me.

God used Gregory in a powerful way in my life. There was
a time when I would have missed out on having a friend like
him because of my arrogance and critical spirit. Gregory is a
recovering homosexual, and I once hated homosexuals. I'm
not talking about "hate the sin and love the sinner"; I'm talking
about a deep-seated hatred, an unwillingness to see them as
human beings. Incidentally, this was not homophobia, because
I had no attitude problem with lesbians.

I know the reason. When I was eight years old I was
sexually abused by two teenage boys who performed homosexual acts on each other as they abused me. They hurt me, and
they were wrong, of course. But I was wrong to expand my
hatred of them and what they did to me to include an entire
category of human beings. God shed His light of truth on that

part of my life, and I understood why I hated them. But I still hated them.

My attitude changed the day I met Gregory and heard him read the first words of the next chapter. He begins, "All I ever wanted was my daddy." Tears of recognition and identification began to flow. That's all I ever wanted too.

My little girl stood with Gregory's little boy at the threshold of a gay bar, looking for Daddy. God touched my heart and used my tears to melt away my arrogance and critical spirit and transform them into acceptance and compassion. I know that in the eyes of God, judgmentalism is as bad as any other sin.

I thank God for the beautiful person Gregory is, for his gift of being transparent, and for the way the Lord has used him in my life.

Recovering: Intimacy with Others

9

Carry each other's burdens, and in this way you will fulfill the law of Christ.   (Galatians 6:2)

All I ever wanted was my daddy. My desperate, fierce cry for my father's love and attention really began to manifest itself about fifteen years ago when I was twelve. At this point in my life I felt completely disconnected from the world. I had no friends, and my two older brothers and parents were so wrapped up in themselves, they didn't even know I existed. "Somebody please notice me, love me, and pay attention to me," was my cry.

One day I noticed a garment of my mother's that I hadn't seen in many years. I instantly felt very drawn to it. Somehow this was a part of my past. My initial feelings upon seeing this garment were panic, great sexual attraction, and association with my father. Obsession demanded I have it. My behavior soon turned into compulsive masturbation into the garment. Fulfillment!

I had finally found connection and safety in something I could call my own. This garment loved me, had time for me, and somehow connected me with Dad and other men like him. I no longer felt alone and abandoned, but my compulsive behavior grew more intense. Since this one garment was not enough to fill my need, I began compulsively searching stores to find more of the same item until my collection had grown to about twenty-five.

I now felt very safe: The walls were up, and no one could penetrate them and hurt me. Nothing could hurt me except my memories, which were foggy. Eventually I needed old photographs of my father and male pornography to aid me in my sexual ritual. The combination of pictures of my father and garments further intensified my sexual activity. While engaged in this ritual behavior, I felt demeaned, shamed, and ridiculed. This equaled attention and acceptance by my father.

The tape in my head would instantly click on and play the same message from Dad, "You're stupid, helpless, worthless, and a sissy. No one will ever want you. I'm the only one who will have you. You will be my slave and will do and say what I want when I want, no matter the consequences. I own you! I control your destiny. You are not competent enough to make it on your own. You need me, and I will use you to the bitter end. You are my source for sexual favors, and you will give me sex when and how I want it. You are to shut your mouth and perform." I never knew where that tape in my head came from.

The realization of who I was and where I belonged led to the conclusion that my lot in life was to be Daddy's slave. Where did this tape come from? It had to be some event from my past. This was confusing. After all, my father had emotionally abandoned me and eventually physically abandoned me when I was fifteen and my parents divorced.

Falling further into sexual addiction, I now augmented my sexual activity with alcohol, marijuana, and amyl nitrate. By the age of eighteen, these drugs created more intense feelings of panic, loss of control, and complete submission to Dad. My face began contorting into the same expressions Dad would have on his face when he was drunk and angry. My voice would speak out in a similar tone, screaming the messages out loud during sex.

When my fantasizing extended to other men demeaning me, laughing at me, and telling me I was worthless, my feelings of panic and fear intensified. Feeling dirty, very guilty, shamed, depressed, angry, and frustrated, I questioned, Why am I so strange? What's happening to me? After sex I would ask myself, Who was that person who just behaved that way? What is he doing inside me? My feelings were so overwhelming that I couldn't face them or deal with them. To sedate myself, I would start my ritual again.

I still wanted Daddy's undivided, loving attention. Never having had a real relationship with Dad left me feeling empty and starved for male attention. How was I going to get my needs met? The first part of my compulsive sexual behavior was aimed at fulfilling Daddy's wishes and his beliefs about me.

This was followed by a little voice inside that screamed out, "Don't abuse me anymore, Daddy. Tenderly love me and hold me." How could I get that from a father who wanted nothing to do with me? His drinking, affairs with women, and visits to massage parlors and the insane hours he worked certainly left no time for me. I felt shut out. I felt worthless and insignificant in his eyes. I came last, if there was any time at all.

One night when I was eighteen years old I decided to set out and find my daddy, who would love me, consume me, and have me all to himself. Having heard about a gay bar not too far from home, I went looking for Daddy.

But first, there was much preparation to be done. Needing my face to look as young and innocent as possible, that evening

I instituted a ninety-minute preparation ritual, which characterized my approach for the next seven years. I shaved to such perfection that there would not be one trace of razor stubble showing. Eyebrows and eyelashes were combed to perfection. Once that was accomplished, my hair had to be styled — not one hair out of place. After all, I was to look perfect and innocent for Daddy.

By the time the ritual ended I was dressed for the evening and intoxicated with excitement. Fear and insecurity raised my adrenaline level to its all-time high. I was about to throw myself to the big bad wolves.

At the last minute, before leaving my house, I grabbed one of my garments, realizing that Daddy would need this to love me and have sex with me.

The entire time I was driving to the bar a little voice inside repeated over and over, "Daddy, please hold me, please help me and show me how to live. Take care of me, but please be gentle this time." Tears were streaming down my face. I couldn't figure out what all this meant and why I was crying.

I arrived at the bar feeling very confused, lost, and scared. To this day I do not know why they let me into the bar. At eighteen years old, I looked about fourteen. To alleviate my tension, I began drinking beer.

Three beers later, I left the bar feeling drunk and rejected. Not one man had approached me. Another rejection. Another failure. No male would ever love me.

In order not to feel the disappointment I immediately turned to my first addiction, my ritual, and quickly masked my pain. That addiction felt safe and validated my feelings of failure.

For the next seven years, my Friday and Saturday nights were spent in various gay bars searching for "Daddy." It grew to be a challenge. The chase had started. Who could I capture with my shy, little-boy attitude and take to bed?

Each man had the same attitude: "Give me what I want, then get out of my life." I was consistently attracted to thick-headed, narcissistic, macho-type men. Not one of them wanted to commit themselves to me. Not one of them wanted to be my daddy.

During the seven years, the rejection, frustration, shame, and loneliness gradually evolved into hostility toward men. My behavior changed with my attitude. I was no longer the de-mure, love-starved little boy who just wanted Daddy's love. I became very vindictive. My ritual was still to prepare myself to look young and innocent, but I took the attitude that I would no longer be the one used and dumped. I was now in control. I would allow men to approach me and buy me drinks. After building their hopes, I would excuse myself to the restroom and slip out the back door. Thus I would dump them before they had a chance to use me and throw me away. Teasing made me feel powerful and eliminated my feelings of rejection. I felt angry and resentful toward these men and toward myself—this was my way of lashing out and "getting even."

My feelings of shame, self-hate, and depression grew so intense that my addiction became focused solely on acting out the ritual with my garments, pornography, and pictures of Dad. The walls went higher, and I was isolated from the world. I felt like such a failure and loser that the early messages from Dad and what I told myself during my ritual seemed really true. This fetish addiction continued to validate my feelings of worthlessness and shamefulness, and my decision to stop chas-ing men in bars drove me further into it. Completely alienated from men and women, I had virtually no self-esteem, and re-lationships with people of either sex seemed impossible. There were men and women leading normal lives, and then there was me — on the outside, looking in. Alienated from my-self and God, I saw His grace and love as being only for good Christians, not for people like me.

By the time I was twenty-seven, I was feeling completely hopeless, isolated, rejected by all, unloved, totally worthless. Because my behavior was not pleasing to God and the guilt was overwhelming me, thoughts of suicide and prayers for God to end my life permeated my being.

I hated myself so much that thoughts of death returned along with my big questions: Why am I so confused? Why do these garments attract me? Why do men attract me? What hap-pened in my life to make me the way I am? Hating all my inner conflicts and not wanting to find the answers to my questions because I knew that would be painful and traumatic, I contin-ued my sexual rituals.

I was starting to feel powerless over my behavior. It was that powerlessness God used as He introduced various people to influence my life.

One Sunday night I had gone to church feeling very bur-dened. The pastor, Larry, gave an altar call for those who needed prayer. I went forward. While he prayed with me he looked me straight in the eye and said, "God is starting good work in you. He is promising to heal the confusion and bring everything out into the open. All that is hidden in your closet will come out, and you will be set free." I left that night feeling convicted. It was as if Larry knew everything that was going on in my life.

The following week I went to see Larry and told him about my behavior. He prayed with me, did not judge me, and gave me the name of someone who was running a support group.

I phoned Dave, the support group leader, and began at-tending the meetings, but only physically. I did nothing about stopping my acting out behavior. I was so angry that I never even heard what others were sharing.

Life became really frightening during the summer of 1986. Being laid off from my job had made me feel even more worthless. I spent my summer drinking, smoking marijuana, compulsively masturbating, and, once again, having numerous affairs with men. I didn't want to feel any of my real pain, confusion, and detachment from society.

I talked about my behavior with Dave. He suggested I make an appointment with a therapist.

During my first session with Keith, my therapist, I was filled with anxiety and mistrust. God moved slowly in the beginning. Keith and I spent a full two years sorting out the family dysfunction and where I fit in. While dealing with my fetish addiction we began exploring the possibility that I had been molested. This concept was so atrocious to me that I continued to act out in every way possible, subconsciously hoping that Keith would get frustrated and angry with me. I needed to hear from him that there was no hope for me so that I could continue my addictive behavior. Yet, through it all, Keith never gave up on me. He portrayed unconditional love, acceptance, and patience — all those things that God is but that I had never experienced Him to be.

One night in October of 1987, God revealed Himself to me in a vivid dream and vision. I dreamed that I was at a church altar being prayed for by the pastor. Immediately I fell to the ground and came out of my body. As my spirit was in the air, I looked down and wondered who that person was. My body was full of turmoil and fear. Eventually my spirit reentered my body, and I lay there feeling peaceful. At that moment there was a real earthquake, which woke me from my dream. Opening my bedroom door, I stood fearfully in the doorway. Looking straight ahead, I saw a large person sitting in the living room chair. He was dressed in white and looked about seven feet tall. His hair was short and brown, and he appeared very strong, confident, peaceful, and loving. There was a white shroud hanging across the living room wall.

I was in shock! What was this? But a sense of peace and assurance flooded over me. I knew I was safe. Within about thirty seconds the vision disappeared. I went back to bed, praying to God and thanking Him. My prayers and praise eventually came out in an unknown tongue, and I peacefully fell asleep.

The next morning I felt changed. God had assured me that He was really with me and that I would recover. The dream and vision were to let me know that God was carrying me and working in my life. I felt hope and a strong assurance that my past would unfold and I would discover why I behaved as I did.

God then used a woman named Lynda, who prayed with me and called me at home with various encouraging Bible verses. I knew in my heart that my rituals were a form of idolatry and that where idols are, God cannot work. Lynda's prayer was that the power of the idols would break so God could reveal the truth.

One night, clutched in overwhelming fear, I put all my fetishes and pornography in a large bag and threw them away. This step was extremely painful for me. Fifteen year's worth of connection to these garments was now out of my life. My loss was monumental. My home now seemed empty and cold. How was I to live without my rituals?

Then the memories of molestation by my father started surfacing. I became so terrified that after two weeks I fell back into my ritual in order to mask my feelings and memories of terror. Keith suggested I enter a treatment program in order to achieve some sexual sobriety and deal with my memories.

Feeling broken and out of control, I agreed to check into the hospital. Before leaving, my prayer to God was that my time in the hospital would reveal the truth from my past and that Christ would take complete control of my life.

In the hospital I worked with a therapist named Earl. It was there that the pieces to the puzzle started falling into place. Through several hypnosis sessions I recalled one evening when I was five years old. I was home alone with one of my brothers. In a fit of anger, he began to tie me up in one of my mother's garments. Suddenly he heard my father's car drive up. He panicked. Leaving me alone in the kitchen, he fled to the safety of his bedroom. I remained in the kitchen alone, helpless and in tears. When my father came in, he began laughing crudely. Suddenly he became very angry. He bent down as if to untie me, but instead, with great force and anger, he demanded I have oral sex with him and then he raped me. The event was so horrible for me that I passed out. I cannot remember how the evening ended.

I was also able to retrieve the memories of two other acts of molestation. Both occurred when I was eight years old. My brother forced me to put on my mother's dress and proceeded to masturbate me and demand I do the same to him. Later that year, while I was visiting my grandmother, her thirty-eight-year-old neighbor saw me playing one afternoon and invited me over for a Coke. This offer was very alluring because my grandmother never drank Coke, so I went. She asked me to lie down on the lounge in her backyard while she went to get my Coke. Upon returning, she was wearing a bikini. After giving me my drink, she sat next to me and began to unzip my pants and masturbate me. I ran back to my grandmother's house in terror and never said a word about it.

By the time these events came back to memory, I felt enraged, betrayed, and shattered. How could they have done these things to me?

A scripture in the Bible kept coming to my heart: "You shall know the truth and the truth will set you free." Deciding to confront my family with these events, I called a family meeting at the hospital. My brother was willing to discuss the events and admitted that he had sexually abused me. Dad, on the other hand, became extremely hostile, denied everything, and eventually left the meeting when we began discussing his alcoholism. His anger scared me.

The truth was now out, and I felt even more vulnerable. Oddly enough, I felt guilty for embarrassing Dad in front of everyone. He hated me for exposing the family secrets.

In the days that followed I began experiencing my real need, which was for a safe, healthy dad to hold and nurture me appropriately. Inside me was a very broken, disappointed, scared, and hurting little five-year-old boy.

My desire for fatherly nurture became even more real when I left the hospital and had to say good-bye to Earl. He was everything I had ever wanted in a dad and had never gotten. He was so kind and sensitive, yet strong and nurturing. These were qualities in a father that I need and for which I am starved.

My recovery didn't end with my stay in the hospital. I returned to weekly counseling with Keith. I am very thankful to God for putting both of these very nurturing and caring men in my life. The hurt little boy inside me is always telling me, "Boy, oh boy, I want to grow up some day and be just like Keith and Earl. They're the best dads in the world."

I began attending a church close to home and one of their support groups for people from dysfunctional families.

God has richly blessed me with some very close friends who provide deep support and encouragement. In some of the meetings, I had discussed feeling like a frightened, lost five-year-old boy inside an adult body. Some of my friends picked up on this. For my birthday they planned a surprise sixth birthday party for me.

I will never forget that day as long as I live. The amount of time, energy, thoughtfulness, and love that went into that party reached way into the black hole inside me and filled it up with love and nurturing. We played several games, like Pin the Tail on the Donkey, watched Casper the Friendly Ghost cartoons, colored, barbecued, and had a chocolate cake with a large white teddy bear sitting on top.

These friends encouraged me as I said good-bye to my fifth year, which was filled with darkness and emptiness, and helped me celebrate my new year. I am now six years old emotionally. I know that God will continue to work in my life and help me to grow emotionally stronger.

ﻉ٨

Thank You, God, for the caring people you have, and will, put in my life. I glorify your name as I see bondages breaking and healing taking place. Mold me into the strong, confident Christian man that you created me to be. Bless me with children of my own, and prepare me to love and nurture them as you would. Help me to accept my past, work through my guilt and shame, and accept your love and forgiveness. With my efforts and yours, bring my inner child to life, and use me to help others and glorify your name. Amen.

Knowing Jeanie has been a blessing for me and for many others, not only because of the special person she is, but also because she has been working on her recovery for twelve years.

When I had my first memories, I remember thinking, Hmmm, this should take six weeks to fix, six months at the outside. As I begin my third year of recovery, with memories still emerging, I realize that this journey is not a destination but a lifelong process.

Knowing Jeanie, hearing her share her past growth, and seeing her continue to grow, gives me hope. She gives me strength to continue on my own journey of growth and discover, leaning always on the Lord.

Recovering: Intimacy with Self

10

For God, who said "Let the light shine out of the darkness" made his light shine in our hearts.
(2 Corinthians 4:6)

I sat alone in my rocking chair. This had become my safe place. On this warm spring afternoon the sun was shining through the window behind me. Pictures of my children gently looked down at me from the nearby bookshelf. In this safe place I once again met my inner child, who had hidden for so long. As I sat rocking and crying I seemed to lose myself in the pain, fear, and hopelessness of my child within. For that time, I became her.

I had spent years learning to deal cognitively with having been abused, but inwardly I often felt bad, inadequate, helpless. Through regressive therapy, I had learned that these were the feelings of the young abused child within me. I was just learning to talk about her, and she easily reverted back to the old feelings.

That afternoon I had attempted to come out of my false, pretending, confident self and share these fragile feelings with a church leader. She responded, "I thought you were further along than that." Hurt drove me deeper into the feelings of hopelessness. Maybe I hadn't really changed; maybe I never would.

As I sat in the rocker and allowed myself to feel her pain and fear something different happened. Instead of running away or pretending, I listened. My child shared more. Listening to her pain and staying with her, I felt comforted, loved and accepted. I felt it was safe that day to feel weak, inadequate, and hopeless.

As I came back to my adult self, I knew that my inner child was part of me but not all of me. Another real part within felt safe and strong and knew how to be loving and accepting.

I was protective of myself for a while afterward and continued to hide my weakness from the church leader. But there were safe places for me to share these hidden parts of me. I could share with my God, my trusted friends, and my counselor.

Because of their love and support, in time I was even able to go back to the church leader and share with her. I told her about my false, pretending self and my desire to be real. I shared with her the pain of being real, the fear of rejection and the loneliness of separation that I felt when I was not real with her. Tears welled up in her eyes as we continued to share. Our openness and honesty brought us closer together, and I didn't feel as lonely. We prayed with each other, and I didn't feel as weak and afraid.

I was reminded of two passages in the Bible. In one Jesus tells us to become as little children, and in another we are to disclose ourselves and pray for one another. That day I knew the value of both. Little children know that they are weak and need others to love, protect, and feed them. My inner child had been hurt and was afraid to be weak and needy. She created a make-believe world in which she pretended to be so strong and self-sufficient that she didn't need anyone. Sometimes this pretending worked. Most of the time it felt like serving a sentence in a solitary dungeon.

I was not able to achieve intimacy with my inner child alone. I needed to learn trust and acceptance through a process of others modeling these for me. My trusted friend Cindy was one of these people. She is on her own journey of healing. People like her and my counselor helped me to go back into the terror of the night and face the memories and feelings that have hidden away parts of me. When I trust God and those He uses, his truth exposes the lies that have kept me in bondage to fear and my false self. In him I am strong, worthy, and lovable.

Eleven years ago when I was in my early thirties, I began to share with a few people that I had been sexually abused repeatedly by my father, his brother, and my half brother from infancy to nineteen years of age. At that time there weren't any groups that I knew of for adults molested as children, and very few adults were talking about abuse, so I seldom found it safe to share my feelings. But it was becoming increasingly difficult to deny them.

As a teacher, I had reported on several students whom I knew were being molested. As I searched for someone to help them and their families, I found a group for mothers of incest victims. I began attending the group because I wanted to help my students, but somewhere inside I knew that I too wanted help I was too afraid to ask for. I led the group to believe that I had resolved my issues.

The counselor in this group supported my defense by complimenting me often on how well I had dealt with my abuse and how strong and productive I had become. I agreed and was pleased with myself, but sometimes I felt like a phony.

I was not aware that I had a hurting, raging child within. I was only aware of her feelings and these frightened me. For several months I struggled to hide and to deny the rage that I felt toward the mothers in this group. I was outraged by their failure to protect their children. I felt angry when they focused week after week on their own pain. I wanted them to focus on their children's pain — and my own.

What I didn't understand then was that they needed to deal with their pain and I needed to focus on mine. As I bottled up my anger, I was angry and upset more often at home, so, with my husband's encouragement, I soon quit the group.

I was trying to run away from my anger, but a turning point came for me one day when my father came to my house yelling and threatening me. Throughout my childhood the family rule was: "be quiet if Dad yells and threatens or you will provoke his violent, unpredictable rage. And if you are beaten, stand still and take it because a wimpering coward makes him even angrier and you will get a worse beating." At first I felt afraid and helpless, like a kid who couldn't stop him from beating me. My impulse was to run. I remembered the time he beat my husband so badly that we both ran, fearing for our lives. I felt like passing out. But suddenly I got angry.

The adrenaline from the anger must have blocked my fear. Almost without realizing it, I decided that I wasn't going to take any more abuse. I ordered my father to leave my home and not come back.

I screamed, "I don't want to see you anymore" and left the room. He started to come after me, but my husband stepped between us and tried to calm him.

From my bedroom I could hear my husband say, "She'll calm down, she didn't mean it." I tried to convince my husband that I *did* mean it. He tried to calm me down in the way he knew best; he took me to bed. I usually enjoyed sex with him and seldom said no, but this day was different. I had just stood up to my father, and right now I didn't enjoy my husband touching me. I said no. I didn't see my dad for two and a half years, but I wasn't ready to be that confrontational with my husband. I went back to my usual way of comforting us both — I denied my feelings.

This strong denial of my feelings came out in yet another way. I unconsciously decided to become stronger, more productive, and very independent. I became so busy taking care of others that I seldom had time to feel or to think about my own needs. I set out to become a super-mom, a perfect wife, and teacher of the year. I became a workaholic.

Workaholism is like other addictions. It takes an increasing dose to dull the feelings. In time I found myself sleeping less than four hours a night; once or twice a month I wouldn't sleep at all. These manic-like episodes would be countered by periods of depression that over time intensified and increased in duration.

This up-and-down race to escape my feelings lasted several years. I didn't pay attention to the danger signs of burnout or question whether I was headed for a breakdown. My body was taking longer and longer to recover from frequent accidents and illnesses. Finally I hurt my back in an accident that confined me to my bed for six weeks, then forced me to give up teaching and most physical activity for months.

During this period my husband began staying away from home more. I blamed myself for being "no fun to be around." When he did come home, many times hours would go by before he would come in to see me. Often when he came to bed I'd smell alcohol on his breath and get mad. But I expressed none of this anger. I was scared. I was trapped in bed and couldn't run away from my feelings.

Pills helped mask the physical pain, but the emotional pain would not be masked. When all I could think of was suicide, I started counseling.

My uncle had shot himself shortly after trying to molest me and I had promised myself that I'd never be "a weak coward like him." Now I wasn't sure that I could keep that promise if this torture didn't let up quickly.

During these months I obsessively listened to an Elvis song that told of feeling tired, weak, and worn. With the singer, I asked the Lord to take my hand and lead me home through the storm and through the night to the light. Elvis or the writer may have meant to give me the strength to run the race and fight the good fight, but I was tired of both. I *had* been strong. I had endured emotional, physical, and repeated sexual abuse throughout the twenty years that I lived at home. I had run from the pain and fought to protect others. But now I was tired, weak, and worn out. And I wanted out.

It seemed that everything I had trusted in had let me down, including God. Going to counseling was a last-ditch effort to get out of the hopeless hole I was in. Only in looking back do I know that the Lord's grace and love were more than sufficient.

I had an excellent therapist who was patient and respect-ful. He did not push me to face more than I could bear. He was strong when I was weak, and he believed in me when I couldn't believe in myself. I was afraid that my pain and fear were more than I could bear, but when I told him of my fear I would kill myself, he did not seem to share it. He knew that I struggled to find a reason to live, and he encouraged me to seek ways to meet my spiritual needs.

I often questioned if my therapist was a Christian, and friends warned me against trusting him instead of the Lord. But I know that God used him to help me experience love and trust. I experienced letting someone be strong when I was weak. When I wasn't hurt or taken advantage of, I learned to trust a little more. I shared my failures and inadequacies with him. I told him how I had hurt my kids by being overprotective and controlling. He loved me and empathized with my fear and pain instead of judging my actions. I felt a little more lovable.

At first I did put my trust in this man, even idealized him. I wanted him to be my perfect, always available parent. Naturally he was unable to meet my unreasonable expectations and eventually I felt he let me down. This took me back to my need for God. In time I began to see that I viewed God the way I viewed my parents. I was afraid of God's authority and power, and I didn't trust him to love and protect me. I needed a new and different parent for a while in order to have a concrete experience with an abstract God.

As I began to trust my counselor I slowly learned to feel some of my feelings. I felt tremendous anger toward my father and some toward my uncle and half-brother, and I was beginning to express this at times. I was also becoming aware that I had anger and resentment toward my husband because of his drinking and sometimes irresponsible and abusive behaviors, but I wasn't yet able to express it. It was more difficult to allow myself to feel the hurt and anger toward my mother and I wasn't even aware of my anger toward God. This would change.

Lana Bateman, the founder of Philippian Ministries, shared the healing she had experienced after expressing her anger at God and suggested that maybe I was angry with God also. I yelled back, "I am not angry with God!" I wasn't lying; these feelings weren't safe, and I was in denial. I wasn't able to believe Lana for a long time, but the seed of truth she planted would eventually grow.

My friend Cindy had been inviting me to go to church with her for over a year, and finally my husband and I began attending with her. People in this church were loving and accepting and I desperately wanted to believe that they were sincere, but unconsciously I tried to discredit their love. I was critical and difficult to get close to, yet some people continued to try. I was afraid to be hopeful; I didn't want to be hurt again. Church brought back childhood hopes and disappointments.

When I was eight, a church was built across from my house. My parents allowed me to go alone. I heard about God's love and acceptance and asked Jesus to come into my heart. I believed this meant that I would go to heaven and that God would save me from the terrible things that went on in my family. For the next ten years I seldom missed a Sunday, but the terrible things didn't stop. There were gentle, loving people there, but I felt unlovable and afraid to really let them know me. The conflict became so great that I quit going.

In my late twenties I again asked Jesus to be my Savior and was baptized. I thought that maybe I had been too young before. Surely now the Lord would save me from this terrible burden of shame and guilt that I secretly carried. But when I tried to share this burden, I was told that God would not bless me because I did not honor my father and mother and did not have a forgiving heart. I left, mad and scared: mad that they, and God, felt that I was bad and didn't deserve to be loved, and scared that they were right.

Now in my mid-thirties I found myself back in church with the same needs and the same fears. As I thought about the people at church, I reasoned that they must care or they wouldn't spend so much time preaching, giving me verses, and praying with me. But it didn't feel loving. I vacillated between believing that I was unlovable and being angry that they were not accepting. Couldn't they see that I was trying to understand and trying to trust and believe? I was afraid and didn't know how to trust. At times all this was too much, and I avoided thinking and feeling altogether.

For a long time I had a strange attraction to water. Often I found myself obsessively staring into my aquarium, singing "Precious Lord, Lead Me Home" and visualizing driving my car into a lake. For a while this fantasy seemed to bring some relief, but I reached a point where I thought I had decided, "To hell with my promise not to kill myself, I want out!"

I took off in my car and headed for the mountains intending to find relief at the bottom of the lake. There was no fear in this decision. A sense of calm came over me as I drove on without thought of where I was. To my amazement I ended up at a former pastor's church. The fear returned as I heard myself thinking, "Ask Pastor Ron for help, and if God doesn't help then you can go up the mountain and find the lake." Pastor Ron and his wife took me in, fed me, and gave me time to rest. I felt cared for, but unable to receive the food, rest, and comfort they offered.

As I lay numb in bed that night, I was unaware of the plans the pastor and my husband were making. Later that night Pastor Ron came to the bedroom to tell me that my husband was downstairs with my father. My numb, almost frozen body somehow followed him down the stairs as he told me they would help me confront my father with his sexual abuse.

This confrontation was different from the others I had attempted. My father did not yell or threaten. Instead he sat humped over like a weak little old man. I wanted to rescue him, and I tried hard to forgive my dad when he apologized for "giving in to my seductive teasing."

But I couldn't let go of the bitterness. No one saw *my* rage or noticed that *I* felt bad and dirty. Only I knew how unlovable the real me was. I went home too depressed even to entertain thoughts of suicide.

Now I know that the confrontation was premature and that I had a righteous anger God wanted me to release. God was patient as He slowly led me out of slavery to my past. I had yet to learn that God would keep leading me back to the same place in my wilderness because He wanted me to know that I could trust in His love.

Several weeks of deep depression followed before the day that my friend Cindy brought me a tape from church that would prove to be transforming. Only a powerful and loving God could have nudged my almost dead spirit to rise and listen. As the pastor preached about God meeting Elijah at the broom tree, I realized that I, like Elijah, was a weary, depleted warrior who had run away to the desert saying, "I have had enough, Lord. Let me die." I prayed, "Lord if your giving Elijah rest, food, and drink took away his desire to die, then I want to meet you at the broom tree too." It was a simple yet profound decision that I made that day as I prayed and let go and fell into the most restful sleep that I'd had in years.

I felt peaceful and strengthened in this newfound rest, and it was from this place that God would lead me to another turning point in my life. God led me to George Ann, a Philippian Ministries prayer counselor. As I drove to her house for a day of prayer and inner healing, the Lord gave me a prayer to sing. I trusted more that day than I could ever have imagined, and I shared many hidden feelings with myself, George Ann, and God. Through prayer and visualization God showed me His truth in these hidden areas. Jesus had never abandoned me.

He was there and was angry when my father used his free will to hurt me as an innocent child. I saw Jesus hold my inner child when her frightened mother turned away from her. I saw His tears, and for the first time in years, I cried for me. He looked at me as someone beautiful, lovable, and worthy. And I believed I was.

The Lord continued to use George Ann, Cindy, my counselor, and many others to love and support me as He guided me through the next two years of my healing. Eventually I felt ready to confront my dad anew. This time I was able to clearly say how he had hurt me, and I believed myself as I told him that he was responsible, *not me*. The confrontation helped me get rid of much of my self-blame and my fear of my father.

Yet I felt alone and very sad. Many in my family were not supportive, and I had to learn to trust my friends to be my new extended family. Even trusted friends were not always there when I needed them. Through this I began to learn to trust my own inner strength. At times I could give to myself in ways that others had given to me. Often I would talk to myself in a nurturing way, as Cindy did, or in an accepting way, as my counselor did.

One time when I was feeling alone and unsure of myself, I sent my inner child flowers. I gave her yellow roses to remind her of our years of growth and how much I thought of her. The card said, "Jeanie, you're beautiful, loved, and worth loving. Love, your Safe and Strong One." For several days I didn't feel afraid or alone. Sometimes when I doubt, I think back to those roses and once again see myself as God sees me.

In the two and a half years that I saw my first therapist I grew considerably. Leaving therapy was like leaving home, a giant step taken with anticipation and hesitation. Knowing that I could go back helped. Slowly and painfully I continued to face the pain and fear that kept me from trusting and loving.

Confronting my codependency issues with those who had abused me — my mom, husband, and children — and establishing newer, healthier ways of relating was difficult. I still feared rejection. Many times I slipped back into old patterns of relating but I was becoming more aware of feeling hurt, angry, or resentful and more sure of what I wanted. I wanted relationships that were real, open, and built on love — not held together by fear.

As I faced the pain of the dysfunctional patterns my husband and I had established in our marriage and with our children, I became aware of how damaging these were to each of us. For two years I prayed for God's help and guidance, but I struggled with the need to control. I constantly tried to make my husband see his and our problems and insisted that he come to counseling with me. We went to our pastor and several counselors, but he refused to give up his denial. I slowly and painfully came to the realization that I had to let go and let God deal with my husband. I asked God to help me focus on my own fears and codependency issues.

The more I changed, the more my husband attempted to draw me back into our old patterns of relating. When I refused to change back to the old ways, his drinking and abusive behavior worsened. My husband did not choose to come into the new relationship, and I no longer wanted the old fearful one. We separated.

After our separation I went back into therapy but with a different therapist. I went to Tim in hopes that he would help me find and listen to the little girl who was deeply repressed within me. At some level I knew that I was stuck in her fear of loneliness and the pain of intimacy. As we got closer to her I began to have panic attacks.

These panic attacks were not only signals to avoid the hidden pain but actual body memories.

Through regressive therapy with my counselor, I began to remember the night when I was very young, when I vomited after being molested by my father. As I was submerged beneath the water to wash off the vomit, I passed out. I finally felt safe enough to reexperience that night with my counselor because of the inner strength and trust I had gained. As I slowly and fearfully began to let go of my own self-sufficiency, I could trust God to reveal His truth in my innermost parts.

For many years I had experienced fainting spells. My parents never took me to doctors for this, and we didn't talk about it. I taught my husband, children, and friends the rule I'd learned, so they too watched me have these spells for years but seldom talked about it. When I finally did talk to my family doctor he diagnosed them as hypoglycemia, but sometimes I passed out even when I was on the sugar-free diet.

Now I understand that the passing out and the fascination with water are related to being held underwater that night. Whenever my inner child felt bad or dirty or afraid she wanted the relief that she had felt as she passed out in the clear, warm, cleansing water that night long ago.

This was the memory that I had shared with the church leader. Her lack of understanding about regressive therapy is quite common. At first I fought remembering, because for a long time I felt like I was getting worse, not better.

My therapist helped me see the value of regressive therapy. I had not only repressed the memories of that night years ago when I vomited up the icky, smelly fear and pain that Daddy had put inside me, but I had buried my little girl along with her feelings in a shallow grave. I didn't know she existed; that part of me felt dead.

Although I didn't know that her feelings existed, they had haunted me throughout my life. I had lived for nearly forty years with the fear, pain and shame, and fainting — along with the lie that I was still a silent, helpless victim.

I haven't passed out since learning to listen to my inner child instead of pushing her and her feelings away. I still have much to learn about loving and far to go in trusting. There are times when I'm still afraid and feel, "Maybe I haven't changed, and maybe I never will.'" Other times I feel like Much-Afraid in Hannah Hurnard's *Hind's Feet on High Places*, "I know the process towards wholeness is worth it but even after all the miracles I'm still afraid to go." But as I'm learning to trust and love there are more times when I'm now "Less-Afraid."

꙳

The Lord continues to be faithful. As I cry out to Him and wait for Him, I too feel as David did in Psalm 40:2–3:

> He lifted me out of the slimy pit,
> out of the mud and mire;
> he set my feet on a rock
> and gave me a firm place to stand.
> He put a new song in my mouth.

The Lord has given me a new song. Often I find myself singing this song as a prayer as I continue to learn to let go and trust God.

> Hang on, hang on. Let go, let go
> Lord teach me to trust and know
> when to hang on and what to let go of . . .
> Lord help me to know.
> You are my rock. In you I find strength.
> You are my light. In you I find truth.
> You are my love. Like you I want to be . . .
> Lord help me to grow.

Intimacy with others, intimacy with self, and intimacy with God are interrelated. Like the legs of a three-legged stool, all are necessary for emotional stability and true intimacy.

As it is with every step of the recovery process, each individual's experience is unique. So also are our relationships with God.

In her chapter, Lori Ann tells how she grew in her spiritual walk: from a quasi-relationship with a six-foot invisible rabbit to a true relationship with our Lord Jesus Christ. Lori Ann is a gift from God!

Recovering: Intimacy with God

11

Be still and know that I am God.   (Psalm 46:10)

Five years ago my life was as good as it could possibly get. With the help of two Twelve-Step programs I had managed to climb out of a life of depression, isolation, and self-destruction. For the first time in my life I had friends and actually enjoyed being around people. I felt happy, and all seemed well with the world. My Higher Power, whom I chose to call Harvey the invisible rabbit, from the movie *Harvey*, was the perfect god for me. He made no demands, and there were no rules to follow. I didn't have to worry about doing something wrong. All I had to do was think about him, and he was there. I didn't worry that Harvey couldn't help me with my problems, because I had no faith or trust that anyone would or could help me. All I needed was myself. Anyone who believed that God could help was nothing but a weak fool who needed a crutch to lean on.

I hated God. The mention of Him would bring feelings of anger, contempt, and envy. God had abandoned me to pain and loneliness. The envy was for those people I could see who had a relationship with God; they had something I knew I could never have. There I was—God hated me and I hated God. But no worry, I had Harvey and I was strong enough to take care of myself. I didn't need anyone, and I was as happy as I deserved to be.

Then one night something happened to change everything. I went to a restaurant for coffee with friends, as I often did after a meeting, and we talked till after midnight. We usually left together for safety, but I had forgotten my keys and went back in to get them. When I came out, I was alone in the parking lot. I stepped between the cars, and two men knocked me to the ground. I know there was a struggle because I was bruised and cut and my clothes were torn, but I still don't remember the struggling. I know the men were scared off by something before I was hurt too badly, but I can only guess that it was a car pulling into the lot. I stood up, brushed myself off, and got into the car. I felt dirty and ashamed. I was grateful that no one had seen my embarrassment. I cursed myself for being so dumb, for not being more careful. I almost got myself raped, I told myself. All the feelings of self-hate I had hidden away but not resolved came back with a vengeance. I was now forced to look at the truth. It didn't matter how many meetings I attended, how many phone calls I made, or how many steps I tried to work, I felt like I was still a piece of shit who didn't deserve to live.

The attack brought back memories of twenty-five years earlier when I was thirteen. I had been sent to the store for a loaf of bread, and on the way a man offered me five dollars if I would help him find his dog. Of course I said yes; he had offered me a small fortune. I went into a field with him that I had been told never to enter. When we were far into the field he forced me into a shed and raped me. After it was over I got up, cleaned myself with dirty rags from the shed, and went to the store. When I got home, Mom was angry and yelling at me for being so late. I dropped the bread on the counter and went into the bathroom. I remember thinking, She doesn't even care about me; she didn't even look at me; she hates me.

I told no one about that rape because deep in my heart I knew they would say it was my fault, and that idea was already quite familiar to me. In a few days I started to heal physically. The bleeding stopped, and after a couple of weeks the bruises faded and I was able to wear shorts again. On the outside everything was back to normal, but on the inside I felt I was damaged beyond repair. All joy had been stolen from my life. I decided I would never let anyone get close enough to hurt me again. There was too much pain to handle, so I shut down. I would walk around the backyard with my eyes shut and a knife in my hand, hoping I would trip, fall on the knife, and kill myself. I thought of myself as so weak that I didn't even have the guts to kill myself. I was now on the outside looking in — no longer part of the human race. I seemed to be standing with my hands and face pressed against an invisible shield, watching others playing, loving, and rejoicing, knowing that these kinds of things were never going to be part of my life. I turned my back on God, but only because He abandoned me first. It was dumb to have believed in Him in the first place. I hated Him for letting this happen to me.

The next twenty-five years were spent in a deep, dark pit, my own personal hell. My promise to never let anyone close was kept. I didn't make friends, date, or enter into relationships. No one was ever going to touch me again. Eating and sleeping were my only pleasures. I despised myself and my body. I thought I was repulsive, and I became repulsive. My weight soared to over three hundred pounds. I rarely took a bath, brushed my teeth, or combed my hair. My uniform was jeans, T-shirt, and tennis shoes, most of the time dirty and stained. I stared at the ground so I wouldn't have to see the rejection in people's eyes. I spoke only when spoken to because I believed I had nothing worth saying. I lived in my parent's house and was subjected to my mother's constant criticism and nagging. I was scared of my dad's drunken rages and wished he would leave. My worth was tied into doing housework, running errands, and buying gifts for my family. I didn't live, I only existed in a hostile environment and used the rape that had destroyed me as justification for everything. The rape was a hook on which I hung all my misery. My whole life was centered around how rotten, stupid, and useless I was.

At the age of thirty-five, I waddled into my first Overeaters Anonymous meeting. I was angry and didn't want to be there, but for some reason I had promised my sister-in-law I would attend at least three meetings. They started and ended these meetings with a prayer, and if that wasn't enough they had these steps that talked about God. I was not a happy camper, but a promise is a promise. I would put in my three meetings and get the hell out of there. After the third meeting, however, I really didn't want to leave. A part of me felt I belonged. When I looked into people's eyes I didn't see the rejection I had always feared. I even sort of liked being hugged. As for the problem of God, I decided to ignore the steps that mentioned God and choose Harvey for my Higher Power.

I set about doing what I felt was expected of me. I lost weight and didn't drink, but I didn't bother working the steps. In other words, I didn't "walk my talk." I was "self-will run riot." Once more I looked good on the outside and was dying on the inside. During the quiet, alone times, fear and dread would overcome me, and I would remember just how defective and damaged I was. Harvey was no comfort, so I had to keep busy and on the run. Losing weight had also brought me face to face with my sexuality for the first time in my adult life, which scared me half to death. I felt threatened when a man paid any

attention to me, but at the same time hungered for this attention. I was confused; what was going on inside of me?

After the attack in the parking lot, I started falling away
from people and the program. I just knew if they found out
who I really was they wouldn't like me. I told myself they liked
me for my smile and my humor. I couldn't tell them I was dying
inside because then they would know that I had failed at working the program and would reject me. I needed their approval;
I couldn't risk losing it. The nightmares started at this time. It
seemed that every night I was shocked out of my sleep by a
feeling that I was being held down and couldn't breathe. When
I woke up I felt dirty and terrified. Sometimes the terror would
stay with me through the whole of the following day. Killing
myself began to look like the only way out. As the months
passed, I became obsessed with the thought of suicide.

Finally, I couldn't take it anymore; I called a hotline and
asked for help. I had no idea what I was getting myself into, but
I had nothing to lose. To my horror they assigned me a male
therapist. How could they be so insensitive! No matter, I told
myself, I could suffer through because it would only take a few
weeks. But after a few group meetings I realized I had fallen
into a Christian therapy group. No problem, I just told Keith
(my therapist) to keep God to himself. All I wanted to do was
lose weight and be happy. Simple enough!

Even though I hated Keith and I hated therapy, something
inside of me kept pulling me back each week. I figured it must
be this inner child Keith kept talking about. I wondered if
being in Christian therapy was the same as being in church; in
church there were words that couldn't be spoken and certain
things one didn't talk about. Keith let me know that there wasn't
anything I couldn't say. I became curious about God and started
asking Keith questions about Him. Sometimes Keith would use
Bible stories to help explain what was going on with me. I

could identify with Job's struggling through the night, for example. I looked forward to the stories for two reasons: first, because I enjoyed them and they did help, and second, because when he was telling them he wasn't asking what I was feeling. I thought that was a trick question, because I never knew the answer. After a time, I purchased a Bible to check whether everything Keith was saying about God was true. Then, because I had spent the money on it, I decided I might as well read it.

As my therapy continued, I began to struggle with new memories of physical and emotional abuse. My body was remembering the pain from the beatings my Dad used to give me. The feeling of his fist slamming into my small, defenseless body haunted me. The times Dad sent me to the dinner table, with the threat that if I ate anything he would beat me, also haunted me. I would sit there hungry, but afraid to eat. He would threaten to kill me if I told anyone what he was doing to me. I had to wear long-sleeve shirts and long pants in the summer to hide the bruises. Dad constantly threatened to send me away if I wasn't good. Being sent away from my family terrified me, but I was only six years old and I couldn't seem to figure out what good was.

Mom was always angry, always screaming and yelling. She didn't like to see to it that I was bathed or that my hair was brushed. She didn't like being close to me. She never protected me from Dad. There was so much more, that I began to wonder how I lived through it all. I couldn't believe that my parents could have done such terrible things to me. I must be wicked to be making up such lies; my parents loved me. I was the bad one—not them. Though my inner child knew it was true and was showing me all her pain and humiliation, I remained angry and confused.

One morning as I was crossing the street to work, all my feelings of pain, abandonment, and humiliation overwhelmed me. I silently, desperately, called to God for help. I looked down, and there in the road was a marble. I picked it up knowing it was God's way of saying you're going to be OK, I'm here for you. The next few days were quiet and restful because God was holding the memories and feelings until I was strong enough to have them back. That day I started to realize that God cared about me, and that He wouldn't give me any more to deal with than He and I could handle.

After the physical and emotional abuse, I started remembering the sexual abuse. At first, all I remembered was a hand between my legs. I didn't know whose it was or whether it was real. My body was remembering the touches and the pain. I thought I was going crazy. Then one afternoon all the bits and pieces came together in a flood of memories. When I was six, a neighbor man would take my clothes off and touch me. When I was seven, my father violently raped me, and he continued to sexually abuse me for two more years. When I was nine, my brother raped me. It was when I was thirteen that the stranger raped me in a field.

I became obsessed with the abuse. The pain of remembering seemed more than I could handle. I felt like a little girl who was being beaten and was crying out for help, but no sound came from my mouth. I wanted to tell everyone what had happened to me. I wanted to explain that this is why I'm so bad, but I couldn't say anything because it was "all my fault." Keith said it wasn't, but I didn't believe him. Keith wasn't there; he didn't know. I must have done something horrible to deserve such punishment. All I wanted to do was die, but this battered little girl inside of me desperately wanted to live. The feelings overwhelmed me. I couldn't concentrate on work; I couldn't sleep. After a week of this, as I was lying in bed crying, knowing I couldn't take much more, my little girl cried out to God, "Please help me!" I felt God's gentle hand brush the damp hair from my hot forehead. Then peace spread through me and I fell off to sleep. In the morning I woke up feeling rested. That morning I got on my knees and asked God, "Will you take me as one of your children?"

I told Keith what had happened, and he suggested I talk to God about my anger toward Him.

I said, "Why should I talk to God? He knows everything already; I wouldn't be telling Him anything new."

Keith explained that God likes to have His children talk to Him. I thought, "I can do that," so now I talk to God all the time.

Talking to God has its problems; we don't always agree. Once God asked me to take a step of faith I didn't want to take because I was frightened. God was getting a little pushy on this and I was getting angry. I screamed at him, "How dare you ask me to walk through my fear. After all, what do you know about fear? You're God."

Very calmly he answered, "I know about fear; I sweated blood in the garden." Now I know that He never asks me to walk through anything that He hasn't walked through before me.

I had hated myself for so long I didn't believe that anyone could care for me. I would start to let my wall down to let God close, but when I started feeling His love and acceptance, I would start to cry and push Him away. It was a long time before I could let God get close enough to show His love. At times I still don't feel very lovable and I pull away, but He understands; He knows the pain. When I first started to learn about God I would ask, "How do you get to know God? What does it feel like?" People would try to answer, but I couldn't understand.

Today, I have a personal relationship with God, and I know that it is one of those things that you have to experience to understand. Another thing would stand my hair on end — the words from a song, "perfect submission." I hated the word *submission;* after all it was my submission that got me into trouble. I was never going to submit to anyone again. God is patient with me, and I'm beginning to understand why these words were written.

Developing a personal relationship with God has been particularly difficult because of all my incest issues. I came to God as a small, battered, half-dead little girl. My heavenly Father took me in and started to heal me. Sometimes the pain is so bad I tell Him to get away and not touch me, but He understands and is always gentle with me. The healing is slow because the wounds are deep and they have to heal one layer at a time. Sometimes I get impatient and angry and want God to snap his fingers and make it all better. The next minute I'm a tough little girl who wants to do it all herself. Then there are the good times — when I walk through the fear and come out on the other side. I feel good then because I know God, my perfect Father, is smiling at me.

I still have a lot of healing to do. There are issues of anger and pain that I haven't even looked at yet. Most of the time I still don't believe it wasn't my fault. I still have days when fear covers me like a blanket and I can see no reason for living. Sometimes I almost believe I'm making the whole mess up. But I have learned the most important thing, that God is my heavenly Father and He will always be there for me.

Today my life is full of miracles, but the biggest miracle isn't that God speaks to me; He has been with me since the day I was conceived. The miracle is that today I am able to listen to Him, and when there are marbles in the road, I bend to pick them up.

કહ

Father, please help me to remember that you're always with me. When the pain gets so bad that there is nothing but darkness, remind me to open my eyes so I can be led by your light. When my load gets so heavy I can't go on, help me to loosen my grip so you can help. When the voices in my head rise to a deafening roar, help me to understand that they can no longer hurt me. When I'm feeling unlovable, help me to accept your unconditional love. When life feels hopeless and it seems useless to go on, let me hear your gentle encouragement. When I'm feeling hateful and angry, help me to know you understand the pain behind the anger. When I'm feeling bitter about the past and doubtful about the future, teach me to enjoy where I am today. On the days when the gray skies look blue, and there is a song in my heart, let me remember that you brought me through my darkest night.

Lodean is the first incest survivor I ever met. She is chronologically younger than I am, but she is my older sister in the Lord.

She spoke at the first Twelve-Step meeting I attended after that Sunday in church when my memories first returned. Like a beacon of light shining in the darkness, she shared her deep trust in Jesus. As I sat on that cold metal chair, my legs curled up, clutching my bear and rocking to comfort my inner child, her words were like salve to my wounds.

Later our paths crossed several times. As more incest memories returned for me, ritual abuse memories began surfacing for her. On the phone, we cried and prayed together.

One time stands out in my memory. I had spent several hours in a gut-wrenching feeling memory, and I was wiped out. When Lodean called, I could tell she was in a bad place.

Jesus, I prayed, there's none of me left, so you be here. In that way the Lord works, which can only be called miraculous, I was able to listen to her, to be there for her and to pray with her. Praise God that He was able to use me in this way, for this person who had helped me so much. After I got off the phone with Lodean, I felt lifted up.

*In letting go and letting God, my own burden had lifted.
To me, this is the miracle of recovery and the heart of Twelve-
Step programs: that we can be there for each other as wounded
healers.*

LODEAN

Sharing
Recovery:

Wounded Healers

12

You are the light of the world. . . . Let your light shine
before men.   (Matthew 5:14–16)

For the first time in years we were all together, all my
sisters and brothers — most of them my abusers. In order to
survive my confused emotions, I shut down. I had become an
expert at shutting off feelings in my childhood of pain, and I
knew I couldn't afford to feel now.

My mother had been very ill with emphysema, but I hadn't
expected her to die so soon. I had just talked with her on
Mother's Day and had planned to surprise her by visiting on
Memorial Day weekend, but she died early that week.

Our relationship had been good and growing better in
the last few months. She understood my need to break off from
the family. I wanted to visit and let her see how happy I was
because of my recovery. I wanted to touch her and let her know
I had forgiven her for not protecting me as a child.

Questions still entered my mind though. Why did she
drink so much? How could she let her own children, my own
flesh and blood, torment me and sexually abuse me? Where
was my father? Where was God?

According to Step Nine of my recovery programs — one for incest, one for being the child of an alcoholic, and one for being a compulsive overeater and bulimic — I had written a letter of amends to my mother. We had discussed it during our last conversation.

The Twelve Steps of my recovery programs had brought me back to depending on God, but I was still confused by spiritual matters. Part of me knew that God's power and love was in action. But a small part of me hated God for not allowing me to see her one last time.

As I drove up Interstate 5, my mind was full of memories, and I prayed, "Jesus help me survive my family." As I saw the windmill off to the side of the highway, I cried. It was a landmark that signified entering Northern California, or being almost home. By the time I arrived, most of the funeral arrangements were complete. I was to learn later that my mother had planned her own funeral and told two church members she was going home to be with the Lord.

Once again I was in a chaotic environment, among child abusers, drug addicts, alcoholics, ex-cons, and schizophrenics — all my family members for whom I had prayed daily since starting my recovery. I had one year in Twelve-Step programs, and I felt strong and sane. I relied on God, but I still had a problem with churches and religion.

My parents took us to church when I was young. But they left the church and later returned when I was in junior high school. My parents were alcoholics and compulsive gamblers during most of my childhood.

I accepted Christ as a teenager, but I didn't begin to develop a personal relationship with Him until I was in college. As a child, I would pray to wake up in another family, and when that didn't happen, I would pray not to wake up at all. When that didn't happen, I just prayed for help. My brothers and sisters made me feel bad and dirty. After my family started to go to church, I would sit there and feel like sin—not like a sinner, but like I *was* sin.

Throughout the funeral and my entire stay at home, I was in a state of shock. I was numb. I had remembered a lot of the incest, but much of my childhood was still blacked out. Some things were too painful to remember until after my mother's death.

I took care of myself by staying with a friend instead of in my father's house. I took my teddy bear to comfort me and my inner children—the little ones who had suffered the pain and who held my memories for me. People stared at me. Here I was, a grown woman with a teddy bear, holding onto him through the funeral. If people were concerned about that, I didn't care. I needed something familiar and safe. I could not depend on my family for that. In the last year, people in my programs had become my real family. Some of them sent cards and flowers, and many kept me in their prayers.

I viewed my mother's body before the day of the funeral; she looked peaceful, asleep, and I talked to her and told her how much I loved her. I touched her without fear. I missed my mommy.

My mother died of emphysema, alcoholism, and stress. Although she was a Christian, she continued to deteriorate as she worried about her dysfunctional family. She had been physically attacked by several members of the family. One of her two schizophrenic sons had set a fire in the basement of her house beneath her bed. Yet she still loved them all, let them in the house, and looked after them.

Because I couldn't watch my mother suffer so, I had broken off contact, calling occasionally to see how she was doing. I loved them, but I had to let go in order to survive. I couldn't change them. Although some guilt lingered on, I knew only God could help my family, so I let go in love.

At the funeral, I held my father's hand and cried. He was the closest he had ever been to me. A part of me was frightened, but I couldn't understand why. I had so many fleeting thoughts, I had to shut down once again to survive.

My younger schizophrenic brother made statements that indicated he felt guilty. He had pushed our mother down the night before she died. I told him our mother loved him and he should never forget that. He was able to be a pallbearer in spite of the family's fear he wouldn't be able to. He did it for me and for his mother.

We had always had a special bond because we were both incest survivors. Our older half brothers and sisters were teenagers when we were young and had abused both of us sexually, mentally, and physically. I escaped by leaving home to go to college, and my brother escaped by going into a world of his own. I still had to work through my survivor guilt, my guilt at leaving my brother behind. I had to give him over to God because I couldn't save him either. He's become an empty, drug-abusing shell, but I still love him and I always will.

My sisters tried to convince me that my mother wanted them to wear black at the funeral. I didn't believe that. My mother had always told me a person should wear whatever color they wanted at a Christian's funeral but not black — it was a time of joy, for that person was going home to be with the Lord. I remember standing in the pulpit and looking out and seeing people in all different colors; the only people in black were my oldest sister and her children. I remember asking my father about that, and he said they probably wanted to let the world know they were dead. It bothered me, and I filed it in the back of my mind with other things to deal with later.

At the cemetery I felt panic. I thought I would scream if they put her in the ground, and I also had an eerie feeling that I had been to that place before. When my family began to pick up the remaining flowers that were not on the grave, I felt myself go on overload. I felt a memory coming up and put it aside. But the feelings and thoughts bothered me. When had I been to a cemetery or seen people put in the ground or people grab flowers? More would be revealed when it was safe.

I returned home to my safe apartment and to my new job working with children, many of whom had been abused. I hadn't planned to work with children, but when my most recent job ended this one opened up. What did the Lord have in store for me?

My father planned visits to see me, and I was looking forward to them, but there was still a scared little girl inside of me who needed safety. I had been struggling with my eating since I started my new job, and I was scared because I was a normal weight and didn't want to weigh 220 pounds again. I also didn't want to start the crazy binge-purge cycles I had been caught up in before starting my recovery program.

After a visit from my father in July I went into isolation and began compulsively overeating again. I later started practicing bulimia, and in a month I had gained fifty pounds. I was devastated, ashamed, and in shock. I was out of control and dying rapidly from my disease. I was obviously trying to "stuff" something, but I wondered what could be big enough to make me eat like this again. I also did not trust my father, and I stopped talking with him.

In October, my father came to visit me without being invited. He let himself and his fiancée into my apartment. When I came home and saw him sitting on my couch, I had a memory of a man in silhouette in my bedroom doorway when I was a child. I forced it back and went into my bedroom to listen to my phone messages.

I then walked into the living room and stated, "Lock the door on your way out. This feels like rape." I walked out. I was panicked and angry. How intrusive! How could he invade me like that?

Later that evening I was talking to a friend and the memory of the man in silhouette came back. The man approached me. The bedroom was dark, but there was light shining behind him from the other room. He was tall and smelled like alcohol. He touched me, and I giggled. He wanted to play with me. He put his finger in my vagina, and I screamed "Daddy, no." It was my father. My God, he too had hurt me!

Was everyone in on it? Earlier, I had remembered my mother throwing me against the wall as a baby. Why was I so unlovable? I was sin. The one thing I was able to hang onto was that God, only God, was there for me, and He got me through the pain. But why did He let it happen? My bulimia and over-eating stopped for a while.

Gradually, though, I began overeating again, and I couldn't sleep at night. I would feel an evil presence, and I would hear voices as if several people were standing over my bed at night. Prayer is the only thing that would make it stop. I would raise myself up and scream, "I rebuke you, satan, in the name of Jesus Christ, my Lord and Savior."

I told my Christian therapist, and slowly the memories began to surface. I saw people of all races in tan and black robes in the woods with me and my brother when we were little children. There were other small children too. The memories came back little by little.

We were sexually abused: orally and anally penetrated and raped. We were buried alive. We witnessed the killings of babies and a crucifixion of a teenager who they said was Jesus. He was hung upside down.

Faces were later revealed, and they included my sisters, an aunt, and neighbors. They were all satanists. That's why I deteriorated after the funeral. It was time to remember. The memories were bad enough, but the feelings and the fear were unbearable at times.

I was comforted by believing that God would only put on me what I could handle, but I did doubt Him at times. It was now that the real fight began for me. I had to fight a spiritual battle and develop a closer relationship with the Lord. I had to force myself to get into church, and I had to use scripture to battle the strong desire to kill myself. As a child, it was impressed on me that I would die if I ever remembered or if I ever told.

Only the blood of Jesus could get me through the darkness. Denial was my initial reaction, but that was a trick of satan. As the memories continued, I came to believe the truth of what had happened to me.

My struggle continues, but it gets easier at times, especially when I totally surrender to God. I believe God is very powerful and real, but I also believe satan is real. Many Christians are deceived. Because they fail to acknowledge satan's influence in this world, children are dying. Survivors of ritual abuse and incest don't feel they have anywhere to turn. As I did, they may doubt their relationship with Christ and may continue to stay oppressed. Incest breaks the spirit. Only God can heal a broken heart and spirit.

Today, I battle satan with scripture, prayer, meditation, church attendance, Twelve-Step meetings, and abstinence from compulsive behavior. I tell others that God allowed me to survive, and I break the power of the enemy by disclosing secrets. I trust God for my life, but I am not perfect and life gets hard and scary sometimes.

I still question why any of it happened, but I also know what happened to me was not because of God's perfect will, but because of the free wills of my abusers. I believe God allowed me to live for a reason, and I pray my story will be used for the glory of Christ. As I do this, I become more whole, free, and sane one day at a time as my forgiveness for my abusers and my relationship with Christ grow.

૨૦

Dear Lord,

You know my heart and my weakness. You know my fear. You know my pain. I ask that your will be done in my life. I ask that my sorrow be changed to joy. I trust you, and I surrender daily to your will for my life.

I surrender the fear of not knowing how my life will turn out. My desire is to be an instrument of your peace and love. I learn to trust you more and more as I let go of my mistrust and hurt one day at a time. I hope that you put back together the shattered pieces of my heart and spirit. Guide me, teach me, and make me into the person you want me to be.

Lord, I depend on you for my life and sanity in spite of my doubt and fear. I ask that you make something beautiful out of all the deeds that were meant for evil. I ask that the pain of my past and that of all my fellow survivors not be in vain. I ask that you protect us from satan's attack, cover us in Jesus' blood, and allow the secrets to be disclosed, because there is strength, peace, and understanding in knowing the truth and working through it. Give us the strength to do this work.

Thank you, Lord, for life and hope. Thank you for healing the hurt parts of me day by day. You were always there, Lord, and it is only by your grace that I live today. Human free will caused me a lot of pain, but your perfect will has given me peace and purpose.

I pray for those who do us harm, for they don't know what they are doing. They are coming up against precious children of God who are protected. Help us to live today. We humble ourselves before you.

Lord, let people see your grace and glory through our witness and recovery. Let your will be done in our lives and to all who read, give them rest.

In Jesus' Name,

Love, Lodean

Conclusion

In re-reading these chapters, each one written by a person who has become a friend, I weep. I grieve the loss of what should have been, and never was. I cry for the innocent children who never should have had those bad things happen to them.

As I weep for them, I connect with the reality that Jesus weeps for us all. We may never understand *why* God allows people to make bad choices that hurt us so deeply—but we know that our God weeps with us.

We pray that by sharing the healing we are experiencing through Jesus Christ, God is using us to bring you closer to Him. We pray that our heavenly Father will continue to use us and to use this book.

We pray that God will take what the enemy meant for evil in our lives, and use it for good. We pray that by sharing our woundedness with you, God is doing that. To paraphrase Amy Carmichael, "Into thy wounded hands, O Lord, we commend this book."

Recommended
Reading

ADULT CHILDREN OF ALCOHOLICS

Black, Claudia. *It Will Never Happen To Me*. New York: Ballantine Books, 1987.

Dissects the roles and rules of the alcoholic/dysfunctional family.

Dean, Amy. *Making Changes: How Adult Children Can Have Healthier, Happier Relationships*. Center City, MN: Hazelden, 1988.

Simple to read introduction to the Twelve Steps for adult children of alcoholic and other dysfunctional families.

Gravitz, Herbert L., and Bowden, Julie D. *Recovery: A Guide for Adult Children of Alcoholics*. New York: Simon & Schuster, 1985.

Using a simple question-and-answer format, gives an overview of the recovery process, from emerging awareness to transformation.

Woititz, Janet G. *Adult Children of Alcoholics*. Pompano Beach, FL: Health Communications, 1983.

Tells what life is like for children of alcoholics, what character traits we have as adults, and how to break the cycle.

ADDICTION

Alcoholics Anonymous. New York: Alcoholics Anonymous World Services, 1976.

Also referred to as "The Big Book," or the Twelve-Step "Bible," this is useful to all who suffer, not just alcoholics. First-person stories deal with acceptance, letting go and letting God, and spirituality.

May, Gerald G. *Addiction and Grace*. San Francisco: Harper & Row, 1988.

Explores addiction, in all its forms, from a psychological/spiritual perspective. Centers on God's grace as the only way out.

GRIEF

James, John W., and Cherry, Frank. *The Grief Recovery Handbook*. New York: Harper & Row, 1988.

Written primarily for those grieving a death, this is nevertheless useful to those of us grieving the loss of innocence or of our childhood. The section on "Academy Award Recovery" helps us see when we're faking it. The loss history graph helps clarify what we are grieving.

Lewis, C. S. *A Grief Observed*. New York: Seabury Press, 1963.

Writing after the loss of his beloved wife, Joy, Lewis journals his doubts about God and his rage. No pat answers, but comforting nevertheless.

INCEST

Bass, Ellen, and Davis, Laura. *The Courage to Heal: A Guide for Women Survivors of Child Sexual Abuse*. New York: Harper & Row, 1988.

The most comprehensive book on incest to date. Many Christian readers have found portions of the book valuable, in spite of the authors' exclusion of men survivors, tacit approval of lesbianism, and New Age overtones.

Bear, Evan, with Dimock, Peter. *Adults Molested as Children: A Survivor's Manual for Women and Men*. Orwell, VT: Safer Society Press, 1988.

A slim book helpful in validating feelings. Includes a chapter for friends of the survivor.

Davis, Laura. *Courage to Heal Workbook*. New York: Harper & Row, 1990.

A companion workbook to the book mentioned above. With its fill-in-the-blanks invitation, this workbook coaxes you to fill in the empty spaces in your own life. Best when used along with *The Courage to Heal*, but if you can afford only one book, get this one. Also useful for groups.

Frank, Don and Jan. *When Victims Marry*. San Bernardino, CA: Here's Life, 1989.

Husband and wife Don and Jan Frank team up to bring their popular seminar for incest survivors and their spouses to book form.

Frank, Jan. *A Door of Hope*. San Bernardino, CA: Here's Life, 1987.

A Christian therapist and incest survivor's account of her own healing process. Scripturally based, with "homework" at the end of each chapter. Must reading.

Heitritter, Lynn and Vought, Jeanette. *Helping Victims of Sexual Abuse*. Minneapolis, MN: Bethany House, 1989.

The authors share their extensive knowledge in counseling adults who were sexually abused as children. Their nine steps are similar to the Twelve Steps, but adapted to Christian survivors. For example, the second step is acknowledging victory in Christ and the fourth step is discovering self-identity.

Peters, David B. *A Betrayal of Innocence*. Waco, TX: Word, 1986.

Not to be confused with an older book with a similar title, this is a good overview of child sex abuse from a Christian perspective. Geared more toward pastoral and lay counselors, it deals with facts more than feelings.

Poston, Carol, and Lison, Karen. *Reclaiming Our Lives: Hope for Adult Survivors of Incest*. Boston: Little, Brown, 1989.

A survivor and a therapist collaborate on issues of trust, powerlessness, sexuality, intimacy, and the healing process. The "recovery alphabet" sounds corny but is helpful.

INNER CHILD

Bibee, John. *The Magic Bicycle, The Toy Campaign, The Only Game in Town,* and *Bicycle Hills* comprise the Spirit Flier Series. Downers Grove, IL: Intervarsity Press, 1983–1989.

For inner children who know we fight not against flesh and blood but against principalities and powers. Lots of fun to read!

Daugherty, Lynn B. *Why Me? Help for Victims of Child Sexual Abuse (Even If They Are Adults Now)*. Racine, WI: Mother Courage Press, 1984.

Addresses itself to the reader in the second person, using stories of victims interspersed with question-and-answer format. Simple and easy to read.

Mains, David and Karen. *Tales of the Kingdom* and *Tales of the Resistance*. Elgin, IL: David C. Cook, 1983, 1986.

Christian fantasy about the real battle between good and evil. Comforting stories for wounded inner children.

Pollard, John. *Self Parenting*. Malibu, CA: Generic Human Studies Publishers, 1987.

A valuable workbook to help the reader get in touch with the inner child. Must reading for those who have not yet "become as little children." Beautifully illustrated.

Sanford, Doris. *I Can't Talk About It*. Portland, OR: Multnomah Press, 1986.

Beautifully illustrated picture book for children tells the story of a little girl being abused who has never told.

Terkel, Susan N., and Rench, Janice E. *Feeling Safe, Feeling Strong: How to Avoid Sexual Abuse and What to Do If It Happens to You.* Minneapolis: Lerner Publications, 1984.

Written for junior-high age, also valuable for adult survivors. Six well-written stories about children, with important facts given at the end of each story. Addresses the child's feelings.

Whitfield, Charles L. *Healing the Child Within.* Deerfield Beach, FL: Health Communications, 1988.

Charts, Lists, and tables amplify the text and help the reader get in touch with the inner child's feelings.

INNER HEALING

Bateman, Lana. *God's Crippled Children.* Dallas: Philippian Ministries, 1981.

Although it does not deal with sexual abuse, this book is valuable for its perspective on inner healing and intercessory prayer. Also deals with the "f" word—forgiveness.

MacNutt, Francis. *Healing.* Notre Dame, IN: Ave Maria Press, 1974.

This older book offers a balanced perspective and includes a chapter on emotional healing.

INSPIRATIONAL

Bible Promise Book. Westwood, NY: Barbour, 1986.

A pocket-sized companion offering easy access to comforting Scripture verses arranged by topic, such as anger, comfort, courage, fear, hope.

Hurnard, Hannah. *Hind's Feet on High Places.* Wheaton, IL: Living Books, 1975.

Allegorical story of Much-Afraid and her journey to the high places. A book that is a companion for the deeply hurting times.

MEMORIES

Black, Claudia. *Repeat After Me*. Denver: MAC Publishing, 1985.

If you have the courage to fill in the blanks and draw the pictures, this book will help trigger memories.

Buhler, Rich. *Pain and Pretending*. Nashville: Thomas Nelson, 1988.

An excellent introduction to emerging repressed trauma. Non-threatening and easy to read.

Littauer, Fred and Florence. *Freeing Your Mind from Memories That Bind*. San Bernardino, CA: Here's Life, 1988.

Again, if you dare to follow through with the exercises, this book will help put you in touch with your memories.

MEN'S CONCERNS

Dalbey, Gordon. *Healing the Masculine Soul*. Waco, TX: Word, 1988.

Deals with the deep wound in a man, the need for a father to call him away from women into the company of men.

Lew, Mike. *Victims No Longer*. New York: Nevraumont, 1988.

First-person stories of men speaking out about having been sexually abused.

Satullo, J. A. W.; Russell, R.; and Bradway, P. W. *It Happens to Boys Too*. Rape Crisis Center of Berkshire County, Hillcrest Hospital, Tor Court, Pittsfield, MA 01201.

A helpful booklet for boys (or men who were abused as boys) — to let them know they are not alone.

SEXUALITY AND INTIMACY

Penner, Cliff and Joyce. *The Gift of Sex*.

From a Christian perspective, the husband and wife, counselor and nurse team cover many aspects of sexuality and intimacy, including victimization.

Woititz, Janet G. *Healing Your Sexual Self*. Deerfield Beach, FL: Health Communications, 1989.

Includes discussion of covert and subtle sexual abuse, post–traumatic stress disorder, and adult children of alcoholics issues and a chapter for friends and lovers. Tacitly approves homosexuality.

———. *Struggle for Intimacy*. Pompano Beach, FL: Health Communications, 1985.

Deals with feelings of fear, abandonment, vulnerability, anger, guilt, shame, dependency, trust, and sexuality.

SHAME

Bradshaw, John. *Healing the Shame That Binds You*. Deerfield Beach, FL: Health Communications, 1988.

Integrates the relational and spiritual healing available through Twelve-Step groups with inner child and feeling work.

Fossum, Merle, and Mason, Marilyn J. *Facing Shame: Families in Recovery*. New York: W. W. Norton, 1986.

Examines the shame-bound family system and its relationship to addiction.

MISCELLANEOUS

Beattie, Melody. *Codependent No More*. San Francisco: Harper & Row, 1987.

The book that defined codependency. Deals with detachment, acceptance, feeling your own feelings, and the Twelve Steps.

Bradshaw, John. *Bradshaw On: The Family*. Deerfield Beach, FL: Health Communications, 1988.

Like the PBS series with the same title, this will make you cry and think. A basic.

Carnes, Patrick. Out of the Shadows: Understanding Sexual Addiction. Minneapolis: CompCare, 1985.

The book on sexual addictions.

Gil, Elaina. *Outgrowing the Pain*. Walnut Creek, CA: Launch Press, 1983.

A short, simple explanation of feelings arising from child abuse.

Lerner, Harriet G. *The Dance of Anger*. New York: Harper & Row, 1986.

Subtitled "A Woman's Guide to Changing Patterns of Intimate Relationships," this is written for both the "nice lady" and the "bitchy woman." She shows both how to use their anger constructively.

McClung, Floyd, Jr. *The Father Heart of God*. Eugene, OR: Harvest House, 1985.

Written to help the wounded person sort out his or her images of the Father.

Martin, Jessica. *How Our Family Coped with Incest*. Avon-by-the-Sea, NJ: Magnificat Press, 1989.

Especially valuable for the appendixes "Getting Help" and "Where to Get Help" and the extensive Christian-oriented bibliography. Also includes a section by Paula Sanford on intercessory prayer.

Mellody, Pia. *Facing Codependence*. San Francisco: Harper & Row, 1989.

Deals with sexual, emotional, physical, intellectual, and spiritual abuse. Must reading.

Miller, Alice. *Prisoners of Childhood*. New York: Basic Books, 1981.

Exploration of parent-child reversal, when the child is not provided what he or she needs and "parents" the parent.

Miller, J. Keith. *Sin: Overcoming the Ultimate Deadly Addiction*. San Francisco: Harper & Row, 1987. (Now published under the title *Hope in the Fast Lane*.)

Explores sin as addiction, provides guidelines for "breaking the habit."

Omartian, Stormie. *Stormie*. Eugene, OR: Harvest House, 1986.

The Christian songwriter's personal story about her physical and emotional abuse in childhood and God's healing in her life.

Ryan, Dale and Juanita, *Recovery from Family Dysfunctions*. Intervarsity Press, 1990.

One in a series of eight volumes of Bible discussion guides. In addition to the title cited above, they include recovery from distorted images of God, shame, bitterness, abuse, loss, codependence, and compulsions. These studies make God's word more accessible to deeply hurting people. Excellent focus for a support group.

Smedes, Lewis B. *Forgive and Forget*. New York: Harper & Row, 1984.

Bypass the offensive title and read this book. You do not have to forgive; you do not have to forget. Subtitled "Healing the Hurts We Don't Deserve," it deals with forgiving people who do not care, God, and ourselves.

———. *How Can It Be All Right When Everything Is All Wrong?* New York: Harper & Row, 1982.

Offers the hope of grace in the midst of pain.

Resources

Child Help National Child Abuse Hotline
Box 630
Hollywood, CA 90028
(800) 422-4453

Privately funded, secular referral group provides crisis intervention
and referrals for adult incest survivors as well as children currently
being abused. Toll-free, 24-hour hotline.

Free to Care Ministries
Box 1491
Placentia, CA 92670

Send a self-addressed, stamped envelope for a list of available tapes.
Titles include several tapes by Christian author Jan Frank, a tape for
couples by Jan and her husband, Don, and a tape by Don especially
for men married to incest survivors.

Incest Survivors Anonymous
Box 5613
Long Beach, CA 90805-5613
(213) 428-5599

A Twelve-Step group for incest and ritual abuse survivors. Does not
allow victims who are also sexual abusers. Packets of literature are
available. Write or call for titles and cost.

Journey of Healing
Box 680
La Mirada, CA 90637

A speaking ministry that has evolved out of this book. We are breaking
the silence about child sexual abuse. We will speak to church and
other community groups.

Overcomers Outreach
2290 W. Whittier Blvd. Suite A-D
La Habra, CA 90631

Christ-centered Twelve-Step support groups. Not intended to replace
other Twelve-Step groups, but to be a supplementary program that
includes Jesus, prayer, and scripture. Send a self-addressed,
stamped envelope for booklets available and/or help in starting a
group in your area.

Parents United/Adults Molested As Children
Box 952
San Jose, CA 95108
(408) 280-5055

Secular program for incest recovery. Includes support groups for
children, nonoffending parents, and offending parents, as well as
for adults who were molested as children. Reports vary, with some
survivors unable to be in the same building with abusers. Discom-
fort levels vary, as do these groups. At the very least, this is a good
place to meet other survivors and get referrals.

Philippian Ministries
8515 Greenville Ave. Suite N-103
Dallas, TX 75243
(214) 343-8093

Although their interecessory prayer ministry does not target incest
survivors, many of us have found their prayer for emotional healing
to be a valuable step on our journey of healing. Write or call to find
out if they have a prayer minister near you.

Recovery Partnership
Box 11095
Whittier, CA 90603
(213) 947-2685

An umbrella organization for ministries around the world serving the
needs of people hurting from sexual abuse and related problems.
If you send a self addressed, stamped envelope, they will mail you
a list Christian support groups in your area for survivors of sexual
abuse. If you have such a group, please get in touch with them so
they can put others in touch with you.

Survivors of Incest Anonymous
Box 21817
Baltimore, MD 21222-6817
(301) 282-3400
or
Survivors of Incest Anonymous
Box 15095
Long Beach, CA 90815

A Twelve-Step group for incest survivors. Write to see if a group in
your area already exists or if you need help in starting one. Some
groups do allow members who are both victims and perpetrators.
As with other Twelve-Step groups, the program is spiritual, is con-
sistent with Christianity, and has both Christian and non-Christian
members.

VOICES (Victims of Incest Can Emerge Survivors)
Box 148309
Chicago, IL 06014
(312) 327–1500
or
VOICES
Box 1722
Tustin, CA 92681

Both the Illinois and the California VOICES provide referrals for individual and group therapy, offer mail order books and tapes, and
publish newsletters.